monsoonbooks

PATTAYA UNDER(

Ewe Paik Leong is a member of International Thriller Writers in Eureka, CA, USA. His novel *A China Doll in KL* and non-fiction works *Kuala Lumpur Undercover II* and *Penang Undercover* were nominated for the POPULAR -The Star Readers' Choice Award in 2013, 2018 and 2019 respectively. *Pattaya Undercover* is his fourth book in the best-selling Undercover series. Ewe earned his BSBA from the nationally accredited Southwest University, Kenner, Louisiana, USA. He divides his time between Bangkok and Kuala Lumpur, where his family lives.

Other books by the author

A China Doll in KL
Kuala Lumpur Undercover
Kuala Lumpur Undercover II
Penang Undercover

Pattaya
Undercover

EWE PAIK LEONG

monsoon

monsoonbooks

First published in 2019
by Monsoon Books Ltd
www.monsoonbooks.co.uk

No.1 The Lodge, Burrough Court, Burrough on the Hill,
Leicestershire LE14 2QS, UK.

ISBN (paperback): 978-1-912049-52-3
ISBN (ebook): 978-1-912049-53-0

Cover design by Cover Kitchen.

A Cataloguing-in-Publication data record is available from the British
Library.

Printed and bound in Great Britain by Clays Ltd, Elcograf S.p.A.
21 20 19   1 2 3 4 5

Contents

1
Bargirls of Pattaya

I toss my gaze at the neon sign "Good Guys Go to Heaven; Bad Guys Go to Pattaya" and ask myself: *who sins more, the payer or the payee?* I'm strolling down Pattaya's Walking Street, which is like a colony of ants skittering in two directions, with the warm air stinging my face. Dusk has chased ordinary female office and retail workers home and has drawn out the night butterflies – around me the walls of neon blur the evening into day, which sucks my breath away.

Jet-lagged faces of Europeans vie for prominence with the red faces of drunken Asians, their arms wrapped around their Thai girlfriends striding in step with them. Outside an ago-go bar, a mamasan with a mouth and a chin shaped for gossiping and with gold rings fighting for space on her fingers hollers instructions to her underdressed promotional girls standing on the sidewalk. Hues of pink, blue and red from neon lights bounce off their bare shoulders and tinted blond hair. "Sexy man! Welcome!" hollers one of the girls to me, and I reward her with a fleeting gaze. The smell of stale sweat, hair spray and ylang ylang from perfume teases my nostrils as I stride past the sorority of sex bombs.

At a ladyboy bar several high-heeled totters away, bulging bosoms try to escape the tightest possible t-shirts with the same desperation as penises tucked backward towards buttocks in even tighter briefs. Bile creeps up my throat, and a shudder forces its way down my spine as I pass the *katoeys*. Further ahead, techno from a nightclub accompanies the cold air gushing from its entrance. Inside, amidst brass rails, crystal chandeliers and wool carpeting, gorgeous angels of lust lever open the thick wallets of bling-laden patrons with the fulcrum of flirtatious talk as they pour overpriced whisky into shiny glasses.

The scene continues with beer bars, hostess bars, freelancer bars and gentlemen's clubs along palm tree-lined Beach Road that adjoins Walking Street. I make a loop at Soi 1 to Second Road and head back in the opposite direction, passing alleys or *soi* that connect Beach Road to Second Road.

In these dodgy lanes are jam-packed short-time bars where *boom-boom* is dispensed in rooms upstairs; blowjob bars where *yam-yam* is perfected to an art and a science by hags as ugly as scarecrows; ping-pong-show theatres where dancers write "I Love You" with a felt tip pen gripped in their genitalia; gay go-go bars where swimwear-clad men dance on stage and later raise their bums in bed; and soaplands where a frolic in a bubble bath with a sex goddess is a prelude to a happy ending.

However, behind the glitter, glam and gleaming glass of Pattaya's nightspots lurk broken dreams, ethereal ecstasy and, sometimes, tragedy. And behind every bargirl's smile, every coyote dancer's thrust of the pelvis and every *farang's* twitch in the crotch lurks a story: happy, touching, heart-wrenching. I've come to Pattaya to get these stories.

* * *

A gush of cold air combined with the stench of cigarette smoke, whisky and oil from fried finger food hits twenty-eight-year-old Hastie (a pseudonym) in the face as he steps inside Cleopatra Bar (not its real name). He finds himself in a hall taken up by two pool tables, some dozen round tables paired with tall stools, a stage with a DJ behind a console box and a dance floor packed with gyrating patrons. House music blasting from speakers perk his ears and a row of overhead pendant lights reflected on the shiny marble-topped bar at the end of the hall make him squint slightly.

Hastie steps up to the bar. "Siam Mary, please."

The balding bartender scoops some ice into a shaker. Without measuring, he pours some tomato juice and vodka inside. Then he tosses in chilli powder, coriander powder and a smidge of wasabi and rattles the shaker. He pours the cocktail through a strainer into a glass and serves it.

Hastie is sipping the concoction when he feels an arm encircling itself around his waist. He turns his head sideways. Standing beside him is a Thai babe with a heart-shaped face complemented by a small, straight nose and pair of dark brown eyes as warm as melted chocolate. "Hey, darling, you want good time with me?" purrs the babe, her mellifluous voice heating up his skin. "I charge you cheap." Her coffee-coloured skin is porcelain smooth against her black hair falling straight past her shoulders

Hastie draws in a calming breath. *She's too young, too pretty and too desperate.* "How much for short time?"

"Only two thousand baht."

Wow! This is a steal but... "How old are you?" The tone of his voice is thick with wariness.

"I'm nineteen years old plus."

"Can I see your I.D.?"

"Why?"

"To make sure you're of legal age."

"Sure, over here, come." She takes a few strides on heels to the far end of the counter away from the barman and Hastie follows her. From the purse she's holding in her hand, she produces her I.D. and hands it to him.

Widening his eyes for a clearer view, Hastie drops his gaze down at the photo on the card, back to her face and again at the photo. *Yes, that's her in the photo.* He performs a mental calculation from the date of birth. *Hmmm…nineteen years and eight months, her name's Suda Kittuangkitkat* (a pseudonym). He hands the card back to her. "Thank you, can we go to my hotel now?"

Suda nods and Hastie escorts her away with a rush of hot blood invading his crotch and shooting down his legs.

Knocks thunder on the bedroom door, and they become increasing louder. Hastie rolls away from Suda and lies on his back, his chest heaving. *Who can that be?* After catching his breath, he gets up from the bed and steps to a chair where his bath towel is draped on its back. He wraps the towel around his lower torso and starts to move to the door on bare feet.

Suda gets to a sitting position, shivering slightly as cold air caresses her naked body. "What's going on, darling?" She leaps out of bed, grabs a bath robe from a hanger and covers herself up. Then she goes to sit on the dresser chair.

Hastie opens the door as far as the chain lock will allow and peeps out the crack. *Bloody hell! There's a man outside.* "What do you want?"

"You've a Thai girl in your room! I'm her uncle! Open the door!" The shout echoes in the outside corridor.

Hastie removes the chain lock and yanks the door inward. A middle-aged man with pockmarks on the lower part of his face stomps in and stands a few feet away from him. "What's my niece doing here?" There is an accusing tone in his voice.

"She's giving me a massage. She picked me at Cleopatra Bar just now."

The man shoots Hastie a glare through hostile eyes. "Do you know how old is she?"

"Come on, you don't even know your niece's age?" Hastie hikes his chin in a show of confidence. "Suda, please hand me your I.D."

Suda reaches for her wallet lying on the dresser and takes out her I.D. Hastie takes the I.D. and reads out the date of birth: "Suda Kittuangkitkat. Born on 2nd August, nineteen, ninety-eight. She's almost twenty-years old." He hands over the I.D. to the man.

The man takes the I.D. but does not bother to look at it. "This girl is not Suda and this is not her I.D."

Hastie's pulse quickens. "What do you mean?"

The man takes two strides to the door, swings it open and rests his hand on the knob. "Sanoh, your mother and older sister have been looking everywhere for you."

A fortyish woman and a girl, probably in her late teens, step into the room. *Holy cow! The two sisters look alike!* Hastie's chin drops! His gut constricts. The man closes the door and passes the I.D. to the girl who has just entered. "Here's your I.D., Suda."

"Oh, Sanoh, why did you take your sister's I.D.?" The middle-aged woman surges forward to swallow her daughter in a hug. "Go to the bathroom and get dressed. We're taking you home with us." She wags a finger in her face. "Next time, don't ever run away from home again!"

The man tosses his gaze at the first girl. "Sanoh, please show your *farang* client your real I.D."

Sanoh stands up from the dresser chair, moves a few steps and hands her I.D. to Hastie who studies it. *Jesus Christ! Only seventeen years and a few months – not eighteen yet.* His face turns grim as he casts his gaze at the girl's uncle. "She was only giving me a massage. I did not have sex with her."

"It's your word against hers in a court of law." The shadow of a grin forms on the man's lips as he sears Hastie with sinister-filled eyes. "How shall we settle this serious matter? At the police station or at the ATM? There's one down the road."

Dammit! I've been set up! Hastie's breath petrifies in his throat. *Everybody in this room is involved in this nasty entrapment!* Beads of perspiration start to form on his forehead.

As Sanoh crosses the room to go to the bathroom, she flicks him a smug look from beneath her long eyelashes, while Hastie's eyes narrow in disgust.

* * *

Kamon (not her real name) pushes the glass door of the 7-Eleven store open and steps out into the morning sun with me following behind. She is garbed in a side-slit peach-coloured tunic, a jacket and dark jeans. Several long strides across a road take us to the Nakhonchai Air bus terminal in Sukhumvit Road, Pattaya. The terminal is a corrugated steel-roofed building without walls on three sides, and we board our bus bound for the town of Buriram, 370 miles northeast of Pattaya.

Three days earlier, I met twenty-six-year-old Kamon in an

ago-go bar. I introduced myself as Joseph, a travel writer, bought her several lady's drinks and told her I wanted to visit an Isaan village to write an article. Could she play tourist guide? The term "Isaan" refers to twenty provinces in northeast Thailand, and from that region come the majority of the bargirls in Pattaya and Bangkok. My aim was to find out why Isaan girls come in droves to work in the nightlife of these cities. By serendipity, Kamon said she was going back to her village outside Buriram town the coming weekend. So, I made an offer of a "tour fare" for a two-night stay and we shook hands on a deal. Nakhonchai Air operates four bus trips daily from Pattaya to Buriram town, according to Kamon, and we agreed to take the first bus at 9:30 a.m.

Inside the air-conditioned bus, the space is divided into a column of single-seat and another column of double-seats, and a toilet is tucked in the rear. Kamon and I squeeze through the passageway to take our double-seats and after almost the other seats have filled up, the bus trundles out from the station. Soft drinks and snacks are offered aplenty, and lunch consisting of a plastic box of chicken rice is later served. I kill time by watching movies on the video screen at the back of the seat in front of me, reading a novel and watching the lush countryside unfurl outside the window. Eight butt-killing hours later, when the sun is sinking over the tops of coconut trees, we arrive at the bus station of Buriram town.

When we get down from the bus, Kamon fishes out her mobile from her jeans pocket and calls a number. "*Phx, rea ma thung laew,*" she utters, her gaze roaming around the sparse crowd milling around. Moments later, a man of about fifty-something comes in our direction. "That's my father!" He is wearing worn-out jeans, a grey t-shirt with the sleeves cut off and a battered straw hat.

"*Sawadee-kap!*" The corners of my mouth upturn in a smile.

"*Phx*, this is Joseph," Kamon introduces me to her father.

"My name Chaloem." He waves a gnarled hand. "Come, follow me."

Chaloem stops at a Nissan AD van parked at the side of the road, enters the driver's seat and Kamon gets in the front passenger seat. I open the back door with a loud creak, slip my knapsack off my shoulder, toss it next to Kaman's bag and then settle on the faded upholstery seat.

Chiloe steers the vehicle past paddy fields along a pot-holed metalled road lined with palms, fig trees and jacarandas. "That purple jacaranda is very beautiful when it blooms," Kaman says, pointing out the window. Shabby wooden houses line the road at about equal intervals of a hundred meters. At a turn-off, Chiloe steers off the tarred road and proceeds along a dirt track which leads to an open space upon which stand a wooden farmhouse and a separate building which looks like a barn. He parks the vehicle in a nearby simple shed consisting of four wooden pillars and an asbestos roof. Lugging my knapsack over one shoulder, I get out of the vehicle and find myself enveloped with fresh air and the chirping of birds. Around the property are hedges, mango trees, papaya plants and shrubs and beyond are patches of secondary forests and paddy fields dotted with scarecrows and tilted coconut trees.

We cross an open space about the size of a basketball court and enter the front porch of the house. It is big and airy. A grizzled man of about seventy is lounging on a rattan chair. Chaloem says something in Thai language to him, who jerks upright and performs a minor *wai* at me.

"*Sawadee-kap*," I say, nodding.

Kamon kicks off her leather flats. "That's my grandfather."

She enters a spacious living room consisting of wooden shiplap walls and rough hewn lumber floor. Several rattan lounge chairs with faded colours line one wall and there is a wicker coffee table at one corner. Another wall, with paint peeling off, is lined with scuffed cabinets, leaving the centre of the room empty. Two teenagers of about thirteen and fourteen respectively are sitting on a plaited mat watching TV. They toss their gazes at me and return their attention to the TV. Overhead, a ceiling fan turns so slowly that it can't even scatter flies.

Kamon strides past them to cross the living room. "My younger brother and sister." She skips inside a doorway at the end of the room and into a corridor consisting of a wall on one side and several doors on the other. "Come, let me take you to your room." We pass four doors and she stops at the last. "You can leave your backpack in the room first. I want to show you the toilet." She turns the doorknob and pushes the door inward. Inside the bedroom is a wooden four-poster bed with a mosquito net draped over it. Motes float in the stuffy air, illuminated by the shafts of evening sunrays slanting in through the louvre windows with glass slats. I step inside and put my knapsack on the floor beside the bed.

Outside, we proceed to another area which functions as both the kitchen and dining room. The floor is dark gray cement and its walls rise to only waist level. The upper sections are open rectangular frames covered with galvanized wire mesh. The tang of lemongrass whirls around in the air. A woman – obviously Kamon's mother judging from her appearance – is busy cooking over a clay stove fired by dried paddy husks. "*Mae, pheuxn Joseph khxng chan,*" Kamon says, and her mother utters something in Thai language.

Ahead stands the back porch. A wizened woman is weaving silk at a wooden loom. She is staring straight ahead with unblinking eyes but her hands are passing back and forth the shuttle of the loom.

Kamon hikes her chin in the direction of the old woman. "That's my grandmother."

I pin my gaze on the old woman's eyes. "Is she blind?"

"Yes, cataracts." Kamon's tone of voice turns serious. "You want to sponsor her operation?"

Wariness creeps into my veins. "I'll buy some of her silk before I leave."

Disappointment darkening her face, Kamon points to a small hut beyond the back porch. "That's the toilet and bathroom. Don't worry, both are fitted with taps." She starts to head back to the front of the house and stops at a door. "You'll have to excuse me. I like to freshen up and take a nap." Her gaze holds mine for a moment. "So, you make yourself at home. My mother says dinner will be ready at 7 p.m."

Kamon moves toward a gap in a rough circle formed by her family members sitting on the floor of the living room. "Come, join us, Joseph." She sinks to her knees, sits down and tucks her legs to the side. A loose-fitting tunic and a pair of shorts have transformed her looking more like a farm girl than an ago-go dancer. I plop down beside her and sit with legs crossed.

Spread out in front of me is a colourful plaited mat upon which are displayed several platters, a huge metal container filled with rice, a pile of plastic plates, ladles, spoons and forks, jugs of water and plastic tumblers. Kamon's grandfather starts to take one plate after another which is passed from one person to the next until everybody has a plate. Next, the container of rice is passed around and everybody scoops out the quantity he or she wants to eat.

Kamon passes me a fork and a spoon. "Tonight, we have a simple dinner." She tosses her long hair behind her shoulder. "Afterward, I will take you to the night bazaar. We'll buy some pork neck and beef and cook a big dinner for tomorrow. In the morning, I'll show you around the village." She drops her gaze to the array of dishes. "Now, let me quickly introduce Isaan dishes to you." She points with her thumb resting on a clenched fist at a big bowl filled with an assortment of veggies submerged in clear soup. "This is *gaeng oom* – looks like soup but is actually Isaan-style curry." Next, she gestures to a platter of mushrooms with a sprinkling of diced spring onions and chillies. "That is *hetpaa namtook* or wild mushroom salad." She tosses her gaze at Chaloem. "My father always goes to collect wild mushrooms from the forest when he's free." His lips upturned in a smile, Chaloem chips in, pointing to a platter piled with several fried fish. "*Pla som*, or sour fish. Very hot and spicy." I identify the last dish easily. "That one is papaya salad, right?"

Kamon gestures with an open palm. "Come, Joseph, eat – don't be shy."

Leaning forward, I grip a fried fish with my fork and spoon and bring it to my plate. A twist of my fork against the fish dislodges a piece of flaky meat. Together with a spoonful of rice, the fish meat arrives in my mouth roaring with umami. Kamon and I eat silently while Chaloem carries a private conversation in soft tones with his wife in Thai language.

A short while later, the sputter of a two-stroke motorcycle is heard in the front porch which abruptly stops as the engine is killed. A man, possibly early thirties, walks into the living room and fixes his eyes curiously on me. He has complexion like brown leather, a broad nose and lips that seem to be in a grimace. A faded t-shirt is stretched across his muscular body and his jeans have knee rips.

Kamon flicks her gaze at me. "Joseph, this is my husband." I almost choke on the rice in my mouth! Jesus Christ! She never told me she's married. She turns to look at her husband. "Joseph is a travel writer from Kuala Lumpur." The tone of her voice is nonchalant. "He's here to write about Isaan rural life."

"Harlow!" Kamon's husband nods at me with a gentle smile lifting the corners of his mouth. "I hope you will enjoy your homestay."

In the night bazaar of Ton Sak village, Kamon and I stroll past a row of stalls selling vegetables, fish, meat, plastic-ware, rattan products and cooked food. Smoke from braziers, gusts from aromatic spices and the smell of grilled meat make my stomach rumble.

Earlier, after dinner, we arrived here on Kamon's husband's Yamaha motorcycle with me riding pillion. The thirty-minute journey was a butt-bumping, bone-rattling ride because of the motorcycle's worn-out suspension.

"Aha! Fighting cocks!" Kamon points to several rattan cages at a stall. "We can have a cock-fighting show before tomorrow's dinner! Cock-fighting is part of Isaan culture." She moves closer to the baskets which house several birds. "Joseph, why don't you buy one cock? My father can ask our neighbours to bring their best cocks to fight! He can also handle your cock in the ring."

I squat down to have a closer look at the roosters.

"You can choose any one," says the hawker.

At random, I chose a white bird, and the hawker yanks it out of its cage. Holding the animal between his thighs, he squats and gently bounces the animal on its legs.

"See? It has powerful legs." The hawker hands me the bird for me to examine.

I cradle it in my hands for a few moments. Not wanting to look like a sucker, I squeeze its breast lightly, pretending to inspect it. "How much?"

"Three thousand."

"What! So expensive?"

"It's not expensive. A champion cock can cost two million baht; sometimes, even three million baht."

I counter-offer with two thousand baht.

A deal is sealed at two thousand five hundred baht.

"I name this bird Narong," I announce.

"You also need a basket to carry Narong back."

"Basket is five hundred."

Holy cow! This is an unpleasant surprise but I've no other choice.

At the end of our shopping, Kamon and I arrive home with Narong and plastic bags containing pork neck, fresh fish, beef and veggies.

The next morning, Kamon and I stroll to the barn and she pulls open the door which is made of wooden planks in a Z-brace. Today, she's wearing a t-shirt and tight cut-off shorts. The walls are constructed from thick wooden slats and the thatched roof is visible as there is no ceiling. Through the spaces between the slats, I can see glimpses of the neighbour's house, mango trees lining a footpath and paddy fields beyond. In the barn, the ground on one side is covered with gunny bags stacked up to the height of my shoulder, six in a column and four in a row. On the other side lies a pile of stinky manure, and baskets filled with winnowing trays, sickles, shears and hoes.

"See that Kubota two-wheeled hand tractor?" Kamon points at a mud-splattered machine in a corner on the other side. "I bought it from the monthly allowance my ex-boyfriend sent me. It costs around US two thousand." The ghost of a smile plays on her lips. "He's an American and was sending me five hundred every month."

I turn to face her. "Your ex – young man or old man? I mean bachelor or married man?"

"Two years older than my father." Her voice is nonchalant. "It's smelly here." Scrunching her nose, she turns around. "Let's walk round the paddy fields for some fresh air."

We exit the barn, walk round it and traipse down a pebbly path which runs past a huge pond. Dragonflies are flitting around the tall reeds bordering its banks.

Kamon casts her gaze at the tranquil pond. "This pond has a kind of green– err, how to say?"

I squint to get a better view of the green patches on the water's surface. "That's called algae."

"Yes, the algae can be used as food for the ducks and chickens."

Soon, we are sauntering down a footpath converted from a bund separating two paddy plots. We reach the end of the footpath after a distance of roughly four hundred metres and it now forks left and right perpendicularly. Beyond is a plot of land covered with sparse undergrowth.

Kamon points at it. "I plan to buy that land very soon. It belongs to the government. My family can clear up the jungle and use it to grow sugar cane." A breeze picks up strands of her stray hair and dances them about her face. "Last month, I brought my German boyfriend here." She pushes the stray hair away. "In Pattaya, he asked me to be his girlfriend and quit the bar industry. I said he must give me money so I can open a small shop. He has started to wire money to me every month already."

"He was here? But what about your husband?"

"I introduced him as my brother!" A loud chortle gushes from her lips *sans* lipstick. "And Wolfgang – that's my boyfriend's name – believed me!" She almost doubles up with laughter. "He also stayed in the same room as you're staying now. During his stay, my husband slept two nights in the barn."

It is now next day in the early afternoon. Wind blowing in our faces, Kamon and I are trundling on her motorcycle along a narrow gravelly road lined intermittently on both sides with undergrowth, shrubs and shady trees. An abandoned house, set about ten metres from the road, starts to come into view. It stands on concrete pillars and a weathered wooden staircase leads to a front porch. Rotting planks have fallen off in many places in the walls and elephant grass has grown to the height of a man's knees in the surrounding environs.

Kamon applies the brakes of the motorcycle, which slows and eventually stops. Remaining seated, she props the motorcycle upright by supporting it with her left leg. Simultaneously, I lift my left foot off the footrest bar and rest it on the ground to help her support the bike.

An hour earlier, she and I went to Ton Sak village to meet three teenage girls in a fan-ventilated restaurant. She had set up this appointment as she wanted to recruit them to work for a bar in Pattaya. She confessed that she would get a commission for each girl recruited provided they stay for three months. The moment the three lasses entered the restaurant, Kamon moved to another table, leaving me alone. As I watched her play the role of recruiter from afar, it became obvious to me that poverty and recruitment by fellow countrywomen are the main reasons why so many Isaan girls end up in the bar industry.

"That house has been abandoned for five, six years." Kamon points with her forefinger. "The owner's wife was a *sopheni khway* – in English means buffalo-prostitute." She turns her head back to lock eyes with me. "She contracted HIV and infected her husband. Both husband and wife eventually died. After their deaths, their three children decided to leave the village and went to Korat to work. For some unknown reason, they have been unable to sell the farm."

Her cavalier attitude towards talking about sex work surprises me, hitching my breath. "What's a buffalo-prostitute?" The blood warms in my cheeks as I blush.

"Here, there is a practice of renting out buffalos to plough the land because some farmers don't own these animals. Usually, the buffalo-owner's wife or daughter would send the buffalos to the renters. Sometimes, they had to sleep overnight from village to village. So, some of the women would also take the opportunity to sell sex services to the renter-farmers and other men in the household."

"What about the women in the other household?"

"If there is no privacy in the farmhouse, they will boom-boom in the bushes, in the cattle barn or in the chicken barn." A chuckle rumbles from her throat.

Late afternoon arrives. The make-shift cockfighting ring is merely a piece of flat ground circled by a wall of plastic sheet held upright by stakes sunk into the ground. It has been set up under the shade of a huge tree by Kamon's family beside her house. Dozens of people are hanging around the ring, some standing and chatting; a few are nibbling tidbits; and still others, sitting or squatting at the periphery of the ring. The first match has ended but I didn't pay much attention to it.

Now, the referee bangs a small gong he's holding in his hands. It's my rooster's turn. Chaloem carries Narong into the ring. He and a fat guy squat down, allowing the cocks to glare at each other. Then they exchange birds. They gently feel their legs and other parts of their anatomy. Chaloem shouts to me: "He wants an even bet of five hundred baht." I give him a thumbs-up. The fatso and I pay the amount to the referee as temporarily stake-holder.

My opponent's cock is henna red, and is bigger than Narong. Facing each other, they are released. With hackles sticking erect like human hair charged with static electricity, with wings outstretched, with backs taut, they charge at each other. Powered with the flapping of their wings, they hover in mid-air, with both claws and beaks attacking. A flurry of wings and a series of pecks create a blur of colourful motion. Gradually, both birds slow down, as if catching their breath.

Bloody feathers lay scattered in the ring. The referee bangs the gong and Chaloem rushes into the ring, picks Narong up. Narong's legs are wobbly as it is bleeding from the thigh. Squatting at the edge of the ring, Chaloem places the bird's whole head halfway into his mouth. He inhales through his nose, exhales through his mouth repeatedly to refresh Narong with his hot breath. *Dong*! The second round starts. Chaloem again enters the ring with my Narong. However, my bird is unable to stand, and the referee declares my opponent's bird as the winner.

"Yahoo!" Outside the ring, Kamon leaps and punches the air. "Yay!"

I sear her with a glare. "Why're you so happy?"

"I bet on your opponent's cock!" A crooked grin surfaces on Kamon's lips. "Didn't you notice its behaviour before the fight? It puffed its chest feathers frequently, indicating an aggressive temperament!" A serious expression steals her grin away. "Sorry, Joseph, money's money. I didn't want to bet on your cock just to make you happy."

The evening ends with a sumptuous meal and the singing of Thai folk songs.

The next morning, while on a bus back to Pattaya, I cast a side glance at Kamon sitting next to me – her beautiful eyes closed in a catnap – and a surmise surfaces in my mind: any man – either young or old – who enters the manipulative world of a Pattaya bargirl has, in most cases, double-damned himself.

Moments later, Kamon's mobile phone in her jacket pocket beeps as a text message comes in. She opens her eyes, takes out her phone and reads the message. "Shit! Wolfgang wants to break off with me!" Then she turns to me and her red lips curl like rose petals in bloom. "Joseph, you wanna be my boyfriend? Replace

Wolfgang." Her tone of voice is pure and sweet as if from heaven.

Holy cow! My jaw drops.

* * *

Long hair spread on the pillow, Nattaporn stretches her arms above her head and the motion pulls her breasts, as ripe and round as melons, high in her chest. She sucks in an inhale, releases it and drops her hands to her side. Anton, huddled naked beside her in a foetal position, stirs and his eyes open.

Nattaporn turns to face him. "Good morning, darling." Her voice is sleepy.

A faint smile flicks across Anton's face. "Morning."

She reaches out to rest a gentle arm on his waist. "Did you sleep well?"

"Never slept better in my life. After you re-wrote the *Karma Sutra*, I was exhausted!" He stretches out one hand to cup her face tenderly.

The previous night, thirty-year-old Anton, hailing from Denmark, visited Ugly Toad Go-Go Bar and barfined twenty-three-year-old Nattaporn out for a full day.

Nattaporn takes his hand, holds it to her lips and kisses it. "Darling," she asks, casting her gaze at his middle finger, "what kind of gem is this?"

He looks at the ring, then up at her face and smiles into her eyes. "Topaz – I bought it in Myanmar."

"You like gemstones?"

Anton takes his hand away from her grasp and fondles one breast. "Yes."

A muscle jerks in Nattaporn's cheek. "Now I remember: today's the last day of the tax-free gems sale – a special promotion." She flicks a stray blond hair away from Anton's forehead.

"Oh? Where?"

"At the Thailand Gems Export Centre in Bangkok. They've affiliate stores in Phuket, Chiangmai and Pattaya. You can buy the gems cheaply and sell them at three or four times the original price in your home country." Nattaporn manoeuvres to a sitting position. "I can take you to the affiliate store if you're interested."

"Sure why not? There's no harm in going there for a look."

Anton climbs down from the back of the tuk-tuk as it screeches to a halt outside Apollo Jewelry Store (not its real name) in Central Pattaya. He stretches out his hand and Nattaporn holds on to it to step down from the tuk-tuk. Under the warm morning sun beating down on their heads, they walk with entwined hands to the entrance of the store. A shotgun-toting security guard pacing around on the sidewalk nods at them.

Anton pushes the glass door inward, triggering the sound of ringing bells above. Upon stepping in, he finds himself in a rectangular room with four gilt chairs set against a standing carved wooden screen at the farthest end. Separate countertop display cases on wooden cabinets run parallel in two rows along the length of the room and faux leather backless chairs are lined up in front of the cabinets. The place is bright, shiny and spick-and-span and smells of rose from air-freshener. A bespectacled man reading a newspaper spread out on a glass counter looks up, folds the newspaper and tosses it behind him.

"Good morning, sir!" The bespectacled man, possibly mid-thirties, rounds a glass cabinet and takes long strides to Anton. "My name is Kittichat, I'm the manager. His hair is neatly plastered down and parted at one side. "How can I help you?"

He adjusts his red neck-tie.

Nattaporn releases an exhale of enthusiasm. "My boyfriend's here to buy gems at tax-free prices."

"You're a lucky man!" Kittichat casts his gaze at Anton. "Today's the last day for tax-free prices. Please, over here, sir." He moves to enter a gap between two cabinets, strides to a particular spot and sits down. "Please make yourselves comfortable." He casts his gaze down at the separate trays of glittering colourful gems in the countertop display case. "These are tax-free – sapphire, topaz, ruby and emerald. The prices on the tags are in Thai baht."

Anton plonks himself down on a backless chair. His eyes bulge in their sockets as he admires the dazzling display. Nattaporn sits beside him, shifts her chair closer and leans an arm on his shoulder. "Oh darling, these are sooooo beautiful!" She jerks upright when the bells above the front door ring as a pot-bellied Westerner pushes it and enters. A short-sleeved Hawaii-style shirt clinging to his body makes him look like a beach bum.

Kittichat looks up. "Ah! Mr. Alberto! Good to see you again." He turns his head to the back of the store and calls out, "Kwang! Customer!"

A woman comes out from behind the wooden partition screen at the back, moves towards Alberto with the gait of a wading bird and stops a few feet away. "*Sawadee-kha*!" She performs a *wai* and the corners of her lips upturn in a smile. "What are you looking for this time?"

"What else? More tax-free gems!" Alberto rubs his hands gleefully. "My wife back home has sold the first batch at a profit."

"Please wait a while, sir."

Kittichat returns his attention to Anton. "Mr. Alberto's from

Portugal." He flicks his gaze to Alberto and back to Anton. "I'm so happy we have many satisfied and happy customers." He nods. "Sir? Have you decided what you want?"

"Six sapphires, six rubies and six emeralds." Anton's eyes gleam with greed. *Those beauties may max out my credit card but it's worth it.*

Kittichat's forefinger taps the buttons of an electronic calculator rapidly and turns it facing Anton. "Total price is one hundred and fifty thousand and four hundred Thai baht." He unlocks the backdoor of the countertop case, gently picks up the gems with a pair of tweezers and puts them in a small metal case lined with velvet. "We'll pack the gems immediately for shipping. That way you'll avoid customs at the airport in your home country. It's also safer than carrying them around or leaving them in your hotel room. We absorb all shipping charges."

Anton hands over his credit card and Kittichat moves away to fiddle with a credit card terminal at a small wooden table several feet away. He returns to Anton with both hands holding his credit card. "I'm terribly sorry, sir." He bows slightly and thrusts the credit card back to Anton. "Something's wrong with our credit card machine. Can you pay cash?"

Anton returns his credit card to his wallet. "I don't have enough cash."

"In that case, can you buy gold jewellery at the store down the road. I'm sure they accept credit cards. You can pay us the equivalent amount in gold after you've shown us the value on the receipt."

"Come, darling," says Nattaporn, tugging at his arm. "I can take you there."

Ten days later, back in Denmark, Anton dials the phone number of Apollo Jewelry Store on his mobile. "Hello? Mr Kittichat? It's me, Anton of Copenhagen, Denmark." His tone is none to kind. "You remember me?" He cast his gaze on the worthless colourful stones in front of him on his desk.

"Mister, I don't know who you are. We have hundreds of customers coming to our store every day. Therefore, I can't remember every customer."

"Last week, I was in your store with my Thai girlfriend. I just sent the gems you sold me for appraisal. They're fake!" A spasm twitches in Anton's temples. "I want my money back!" Every nerve in his body is as taut as a wire trap waiting to spring.

"Please check your credit card slip, mister. I think you've confused us with another store. We are a reputable store which doesn't deal in fakes. But if, later, our merchant-account statement shows that you've transacted with us, we'll be more than happy to refund you every baht." The tone of his voice is pregnant with smug. "Goodbye." *Click!* The line goes dead.

Anton's heart stutters in his chest, stealing the air. *Bloody hell! No wonder they asked to be paid in gold!* He slaps his forehead with an open palm in helplessness. *Nattaporn's a part of this scam! And that bastard Alberto is just a low-life shill!*

* * *

Poppy village, Shan Hills, 300 kilometres north of Taunggyi
The rays of the Burmese morning sun kiss the hazy mist hanging over the gentle hill slopes, slowly making it fade. Speckled over the upper reaches of the slopes are more than thirty thatch houses of opium farmers. A poppy field, divided into plots by footpaths,

stretches in all directions as far as the eye can see, with the pods and flowers of the plants standing from one to one-and-a-half metres high. The carpet of red and yellow flowers has turned the landscape into a beautiful sight. Her head wrapped in a red turban, eighteen-year-old Thawda selects an immature pod and scores it with a small three-bladed knife. Latex starts to ooze out of the three incisions. She repeats the process with the next pod. Working on adjacent plots are her father, Myint Tun, and her twenty-one-year-old brother, Thuya.

Hours pass and morning turns to noon. Thawda catches a glimpse of men wearing green caps and fatigues marching along a circuitous footpath ascending uphill. "*Hpahkain!* [Father] Soldiers are coming!" Myint does not hear her and she puts two hands to her mouth to holler louder, "*Hpahkain!* Soldiers are approaching!"

Startled, Minyt looks up from a poppy plant and runs on sandals to where Thawde is standing. "From where?" he asks between gasps of air.

Thawda points to the east. "Left side!"

Myint casts his gaze at the dozen or so men approaching at a brisk pace toward him. They are carrying rifles slung over their shoulders. "Thawda, it's alright! Continue your work! They're Shan State Army-North boys."

When the soldiers come to a halt about five feet way from Myint and Thawda, one of them, probably late twenties, steps forward. "Are you Myint Tun?"

Myint takes off his conical straw hat as a mark of respect. "Yes, I am."

"It's time to pay your taxes!" His voice is a near growl.

"But you're one week early." Myint's chin quivers. "I've

insufficient money as I've not sold my opium yet. Can you come in a two weeks' time?"

The soldier shoots a glare through cold piercing eyes. "Pay whatever you can now; we'll collect the balance later."

Myint releases a silent groan from his chest. "Alright then." He jerks his head in the direction of his thatch-roofed house. "Follow me, please."

Three peaceful weeks pass. Surrounded by poppy plants swaying in the cool breezes, Myint holds a pod in one hand and his other hand starts to scrap the opium latex that has formed outside with a rusting curved knife. He plucks the mass of latex off and deposits it into a tin container strapped to his waist by a nylon web belt. As his gaze searches for the next pod to harvest, he sees in the distance a troop of soldiers – some armed with rilfes, others carrying scythes – moving uphill along a footpath and spreading out in different directions across his poppy field.

Myint's ribcage suddenly feels too tight. *Oh no! It's the Burmese Army!* "Thawda!" he yells with all his strength to his daughter working at an adjacent plot. "Run! Run home! Burmese soldiers!" He feels his chest almost collapsing at the effort, his heart battering in his rib cage.

Myint scampers east to the edge of the poppy field and reaches the surrounding scrub further ahead. He clambers over a dead tree trunk and crouches down. A minute later, he plucks up enough courage to peek above the tree trunk. *Oh hell, my livelihood is being destroyed!* Several soldiers are swinging scythes to cut his poppy plants, while a few others are standing guard with rifles at the ready position. The poppy plants blur in Myint's vision as wetness shimmers in his eyes. His face twists in anguish and he lowers his head to the ground.

Several minutes breeze by. A hail of gunfire erupts from the surrounding jungle in the west. The Burma Army soldiers drop their scythes and crouch, while a few return fire. *The Shan State Army-North is here!* Myint sees several Shan soldiers break from the cover of the jungle to enter the poppy field. The Shan soldiers fire a second burst, crouch under the cover of the poppy plants, crawl forward on their bellies, rise to their knees to fire another burst, crouch again, crawl forward again, rise to fire again and so forth. The Burmese soldiers retreat and gunfire gradually stops.

Myint gets to his feet and his eyes survey the damage done. *Sigh...huge swatches of my poppy field have been destroyed.*

Inside his house, Myint is sitting on a reed mat in the living room with his wife Yadana, Thawda and Thuya. A pot of *nangyi thoke* and platters of yellow rice cakes and tofu *nway* are set in front of them. A fortnight has passed since the Burmese Army nearly destroyed Myint's poppy field.

Myint scoops a spoonful of *nangyi thoke* – a mix of dry round noodles, bean sprouts and chicken slices tossed in turmeric and chilli oil – with a metal spoon and brings it to his mouth. "I attended a talk given by a few United Nations people in Mong Nai Township yesterday," he says with his mouth full. "Several of our neighbours were also there. The *nawkyattongya* recommended that we grow coffee. They will teach us everything about its cultivation and harvesting. I think growing coffee is better than growing opium." He takes a swallow and takes a gulp of water from a plastic cup. "But coffee plants take two years to grow before the beans can be harvested." He takes out a box of cigarettes from his shirt pocket, taps one out and places it on the mat in front of him. "So, in the meantime, how are we going to survive?" He opens a small tin next to his crossed legs. "So, I've decided that I will go to Taunggyi to look for work in a jade mine." He dips a forefinger into the tin, digs out a blob of opium and smears it on the cigarette. "I want the rest of you to remain in this farm to grow coffee." He licks his forefinger clean and brings the cigarette to his mouth. "We can start with one plot first." From his back pocket, he takes out a lighter and snaps it open. "Thuya, I want you to represent me at the next talk about coffee cultivation. Learn everything you can, you hear?" He lights the cigarette and takes a deep inhale.

"Yes, I will," says Thuya, his gaze fluttering to his father.

Thawda takes a yellow rice cake from a platter. "*Hpahkain,* I'm afraid coffee growing is not for me." She bites one-half away and starts to chew. "I want to go to Thailand to work. In the big cities there, the pay is good. I will send money to *mihkain* [mother] to hire a male worker to help her work on the coffee plots."

Releasing swirling smoke through his nostrils, Myint squishes his eyebrows in question. "But how will you go?"

Yadana and Thuya snap their gazes to Thawda, who shifts uncomfortably under the weight of their attention.

"My friend has told me that a tiger-bone wine trader operates a stall at the Sunday Market in Langkho Township." She sucks in a silent inhale as if to bolster herself. "He also recruits girls to work as waitresses in restaurants and drinking shops in Thailand. I can go see him at the Sunday Market. Once he has collected enough girls, he will take them to trek over the mountains to Chiangmai. From Chiangmai, the journey onward will be by bus to the other cities."

A crimp in Yadana's brow indicates her concern. "Is the route safe?"

"Of course, it's safe. That recruitment agent has done this many times."

Myint's expression becomes relaxed from the effects of the opium. "Alright, do whatever pleases you."

Yadana's dark brown eyes soften. "Maybe there is an opportunity for you to start a better life in Thailand, but make sure you send money to me."

"I will, *Mihkain*."

The party – comprising Thawda, three other Shan girls and Apirak – trudges kilometre after kilometre on a trail running along a mountain plateau, looking neither left nor right as bushes and undergrowth envelope them on both sides. Occasionally, monkeys hoot and birds chirp, squawk and screech in the overhead foliage, breaking the monotony of the squelch of their canvass shoes on mud and mulch.

A small shriveled man in his forties, Apirak, the recruitment agent, is in the lead, and whenever trail markers are not discernable, he casts glances down at the compass held in his hand. Earlier, he explained to the girls that this trail is used by Shan traders to smuggle opium to Thailand and that it branches north to Yunnan Province in China. The branch trail is used by Chinese to smuggle contraband to Taunggyi.

Thawda is tramping behind Apirak. An oiled paper umbrella is strapped to her back and a cloth bag hangs at the side of her hip from a cross-chest strap on her shoulder. Conversation has stopped among members of the party as they are weary and thirsty after two days of continual trekking. The limited quantities of food and water they are carrying have to last them until they reach Chiangmai.

Three hours pass. Now the trail slopes toward a valley where the trees grow far apart to allow sunlight to bake the ground where scrub grows in patches. As Thawda schleps down the dirt track, gravity gets the better of her, increasing the momentum of her steps, and when some dry earth crumbles under her feet, she falls, almost colliding against Apirak, and rolls to a level stretch some fifteen feet away.

"Oh Lord Buddha!" Apirak scuttles to where Thawda is sprawled on the ground on her stomach. "Be careful – there's no need for haste." Behind him, the other three girls start to giggle, and he shoots a stern glare over his shoulder at them.

Thawda manoeuvres to a sitting position. "I'm alright!" She tries to stand on her feet. "Ouch! My right ankle is sprained!" She sinks to the ground on her butt.

Apirak casts his gaze around at the patches of undergrowth. "I'll cut a branch for you to use as a walking stick." He slips the straps of his backpack off his shoulders, puts it on the ground and rifles its contents. He pulls out a Rambo knife, takes a few strides to a tree and cuts away a branch.

The next day, the party is traversing a valley speckled with dipterocarps. "Let's take a ten-minute rest." Apirak looks down at his compass. "We've already crossed the border." He snaps the compass shut, puts it inside his shirt pocket and goes to sit down under a tree. "We can be in Chiangmai by late afternoon." He pulls out a handkerchief, mops his forehead and flicks his gaze across the landscape ahead.

Thawda and the other four girls disperse to different spots

under the shade of separate trees a few feet away from each other. Thawda unzips her cloth bag, dips her hand inside and takes out a plastic bottle quarter-filled with water and takes a glug, water dribbling her chin. She releases an exhale, swipes her chin with one hand and replaces the bottle in the cloth bag.

A tall girl jerks upright. "What's that?" She casts her gaze around the surrounding scrubs. "I heard something!"

An ominous roar echoes through the landscape, creating a cocktail of frightened wails and shrieks from other animals.

"Oh Lord Buddha!" another girl shrieks. "It's a tiger's growl!"

"There it is!" Apirak hollers, pointing to his left. "It's heading here! Everybody, climb up your tree!" He slips his backpack and shoes off and, with arms and legs wrapped around the trunk of the tree he was sitting under a second ago, climbs up and hangs on to a thick branch.

"Oh my goodness!" Thawda rises to her feet, putting her weight on her left foot, and hobbles to the nearest tree. "I can't climb!" she wails in despair, trying to get a foothold on its trunk. "My sprained ankle hurts like hell!"

The tiger, a young adult about the size of an Alsatian, starts to pad towards Thawda, its tail swishing. Shafts of sunlight filtering through the tops of trees bounce off its dappled coat of orange and black stripes. Everyone up in the separate trees chock back frightened screams, their voices little more than whimpers.

Thawda crouches down, opens her oiled paper umbrella and hides behind it. The tiger approaches the open umbrella and sniffs at it. The beast tries to get around it from the left but the umbrella turns clockwise half a circle, blocking its way. The animal makes a second attempt from the right to round the umbrella and the latter turns anti-clockwise, again blocking it. Now, the tiger manages a full circle, but so does the umbrella. Finally, after going round in circles and half-circles several times, the beast, apparently frustrated, loses interest in its potential prey and goes away.

Apirak climbs down from the tree. "I can't believe it!" He retrieves his backpack and slips on his shoes. "You fended off a tiger with an umbrella! Lord Buddha be praised!

Sitting across me, Thawda crosses her legs at the knees, pulls the hem of her skirt down and takes a sip of her lady's drink. "That was the scariest experience in my life."

I run a finger around the edge of my wine glass. "How many years have you been in Pattaya?"

"Four years." She puts an elbow on the table and rests her head on an open palm. "My first job was in Bangkok – that's where I started to learn English. I was there for five years."

"What's your family doing now?"

"My brother is still running the coffee plantation. He's already married and has several kids. My mother is still alive. She is staying with him, helping to take care of his children. As for my father – " she releases a sigh " – after working for two years in a jade mine, he became a heroin addict. That sort of work is back-breaking. So he started using heroin to find relief from the physical stress. One day, he injected too much heroin into himself and died."

* * *

Kampala, Uganda

Sitting his office, Mao Xiang (a pseudonym) tears open an envelope delivered by the postman earlier. Inside are a photograph of a baby and a folded sheet of paper. He unfolds the paper and reads the hand-written note mentally: *My husband, this baby is your son. He's handsome, normal and healthy. Please send me money for his maintenance by direct transfer to my bank account. I want US$300 every month; otherwise, I'll leave him in the bush to be eaten by lions!* Mao's jaw drops. *Sheesh! She's heartless and ruthless!* He grabs a pen and a notepad and copies down her Bank of Africa Uganda account number. *I better get it done as soon as possible.*

Kira Town, 13 km north of Kampala, one month ago...
"Oh my God! I can feel a strong contraction!" Masiko (not her real name) groans, squirming on the hospital bed. "It's painful!" Her hand reaches out to her belly.

Abbo, midwifery nurse, slips the cuff of a blood pressure meter over Masiko's upper arm and jabs at a button. "If you feel you need to urinate, better do it now. I'll get you a bedpan. A full bladder can slow down a baby's descent." *Odd, why isn't her husband here with her? In fact, I haven't even seen him before.*

Masiko twists her hip slightly. "No, there's no need."

The cuff on Masiko's arm inflates and tightens. Seconds later, it deflates with a hiss and Abbo reads the meter reading on its screen. "Pressure's fine."

Two hours later...
"Masiko, the doctor's here," says Abbo, as she slips a surgical mask over her mouth.

The good doctor sits on a stool at the end of the bed. "Put her legs on the stirrups."

One by one, Abbo lifts Masiko's legs on the stirrups.

"Breath in and push!" coaxes the doctor. "Push!...Take a deep breath...Push!... Breathe in...Push! Yes, it's coming out... Ah... I've got the baby – it's a boy!"

Abbo's eyes widen in surprise. *Jesus Christ! The baby's skin colour is gray like ash! He's has Oriental features!*

Kampala, Uganda, ten months earlier...
Lying in bed, Masiko hears her husband snoring, opens her eyes and turns to look at him under the lights of the side table lamps. *Hell! I've been pretending to sleep for almost two hours and almost dozed off!* The luminous hands of the alarm clock show 12:15 am. Gently, she gets out of bed and pulls out a luggage from underneath. She puts the luggage near her clothes closet, eases the latches up and flips open the lid. She tosses some of her clothes into the luggage, closes the lid and takes her pajamas off. She changes into a pantsuit, steals out of the bedroom and calls a 24-hour taxi service. Then she opens the front door and leaves the apartment. She locks the front door and slides the key under the door.

The night earlier...
Set on the dining table are platters of *matooke, chappati, muchomo* and *luwombo*. Masiko uses one hand to transfer a piece of *chappati* from a platter to her plate. She scoops a spoonful of *matooke*, spreads it on the chappati and snaps her gaze upward at her husband, sitting across her. "Mao, I've something to tell you." She tears off a piece of *chappati* and pops it into her mouth.

Mao picks up a piece of stewed beef from the *luwombo* with a pair of chopsticks. "Yes?" He puts the beef in his mouth and starts to chew.

Twenty-six-year-old Masiko and her husband, Mao Xiang, aged thirty-three, are having their dinner in their apartment in Bukoto Street. In the dining room, the rattling air-conditioner is spewing cool air, while fat tsetse flies are hovering on the outside of the window pane.

"I missed my period and went to see a doctor." She fuses her gaze with his. "He did a test, said I'm two months' pregnant."

"What!" Mao almost chokes on his food, his eyes spanning wider in shock. "You sure the baby's mine?" He takes a gulp of water from a glass at his side.

Masiko's eyes spark anger. "What're you implying? That I slept with another man?"

"I wore condoms every time we had sex!" Mao's brows crimp in exasperation. "So how could you have gotten pregnant?"

"Condoms are not one hundred percent reliable."

"I want you to abort the baby!"

"No!" Misako jerks upright in her seat.

"You must!" Mao slams his chopsticks on the table. "Tomorrow, I'm taking you to a doctor."

Masiko stands up suddenly, causing her chair to topple backwards with a clatter on the hardwood floor. With nary a word, she strides to the bedroom. Her throat is clogged with emotion though.

A year earlier…
Misako enters the bedroom and goes to the side table where Mao keeps his over-the-counter medications in a drawer. She sits on the floor, switches on the lamp and takes out a small round plastic container filled with an assortment of hand sewing needles. She puts the container on top of the side table, pulls out the drawer

and rifles through a jumble of blister packs and small bottles. She finds a box of condoms, opens it and pours out its contents on the side table. Opening the round plastic container, she takes out the finest needle among the assortment. She picks up one plastic-wrapped condom and, with utmost gentleness, pricks it with the needle so that only one side of the wrapper and the condom inside is pierced. *In dim light, it's unlikely the tiny puncture hole can be seen.* She repeats the process with the other condoms and returns them to the box. *When I'm pregnant, I've got him by the balls!*

More than a year earlier...
Mao scans the other tables in the café, fishes out his mobile phone from his trouser pocket and jabs a number. "Hello, Masiko? I'm Mao Xiang. I'm in the café now." He pauses. "Okay, fine."

Five minutes later, Masiko enters the café, spots Mao Xiang easily and goes to sit at his table. About five feet five inches in height, she wears dreadlocks and is togged up in a bare-back sheath dress with zebra-stripe prints.

Mao nods. "How do you do?" *Wa sai! [Wow!] She's Uganda's version of Beyonce! Albeit a notch below.*

"I'm fine." A smile nudges the edges of Masiko's lips and her teeth gleams white against dark skin.

A waitress comes to the table and hands them a menu each. As they scan the menu in silence, a pop song in Swahili seeps from overhead speakers.

"Stoney Tangawizi." Mao hands the menu back.

Masiko looks up at the waitress. "Krest bitter lemon." She returns the menu to her.

The waitress goes away.

Masiko clasps her hands together and rests them on the edge

of the table. "Our mutual friend says you're looking for a contract wife?"

Mao leans forward. "Yes, I want PR status here, so that I can continue to run my business." Fire scorches his groin as he admires her ample breasts obvious in a plunging neckline.

"What kind of business?"

"I'm an importer and distributor – everything I do is legit." Mao dips his hand into his back trouser pocket and pulls out a leather wallet. "I import batteries from China and distribute them to motor workshops here." He slides out a business card from the wallet and hands it over to Masiko.

Masiko takes the business card and reads it. "I see." She puts the card in front of her on the table.

Their drinks arrive and they each take a long sip.

"Does your contract wife need to stay with you?"

"Of course, at least for the first year." Mao's gaze narrows. "From what I've heard, immigration officers will make surprise visits at night to check whether the newly married couple is living together." His lips compress into a thin line for a moment as if to stress the seriousness of the matter. "And they should not be sleeping in separate bedrooms, too."

"What about sex?" Her voice is a half-whisper.

"Might as well include it in the arrangement."

"How long will be the contract?"

"I'd like to start with one year, then see how things progress. If necessary, I'd like to extend the contract for another year, but without live-in."

Three days earlier...

Masiko sidles up to a European man sitting on a bar stool. "Hello, darling, you want a good time?" She flashes a grin that could have belonged to the devil. "We can do it African style!"

"You mean like how the elephants do it?" The European man's shoulders shudder as he chortles at his own joke and then his voice turns cool and abrupt with impatience. "Sorry, I've an early safari to Queen Elizabeth National Park tomorrow. I need a good night's sleep." He slams his drink down his throat, gets off the bar stool and strides away.

The twenty-something bartender walks from the other end of the bar towards Masiko. "Ah...Masiko, you've come here at the right time. I've a foreigner friend who's looking for a wife. It's for a sham marriage because he wants PR status here. He's a businessman. You interested?"

"How old is he?" Her long eyelashes sweep high above her prominent cheekbones. "From where?"

"Early thirties, a Chinese bachelor from Sichuan in China. He will pay a monthly allowance, he says." A half smile quirks up one side of the bartender's thick lips. "So it may be better than you freelancing here as you'll be receiving a steady income." He takes out a ballpoint pen and scribbles on a piece of paper. "Here's his mobile number."

"Thanks, I don't see any harm in discussing this with him." Masiko takes the slip of paper, folds it in two and slips it inside her cleavage.

Pattaya, Thailand, back to the present...
I chug my beer and set the mug down. "Where's your son now?" I pick up a *laab moo tod* and pop it into my mouth.

Masiko's lips upturn in a smug grin. "With my mother in Kira Town."

Masiko and I are sitting in a beer bar in Soi Buakhao across Tree Town, filled with beverage and food stalls. Minutes ago, after a stroll in the colourful Tree Town, I entered the bar and grabbed a table. With a sway of hips, Masiko got off her chair, sashayed to me in heels and purred a proposal in a voice that reminded me of Ella Fitzgerald's. I countered with an offer of a chat-and-tip which she accepted.

I exhale forcefully as chilli scorches my tongue. "Mao's still paying you an allowance?" I gulp a mouthful of beer to save my tongue from further torture.

"Yes. In fact, he's been paying me for almost a year. That's why I can afford to come here – part vacation, part work. Last week, I was in Bangkok." Masiko spears a *laab moo tod* and starts to eat it. "This pork ball's too spicy for you?"

I nod. "How many China-Chinese are in Uganda?"

"About fifty thousand."

I pour more beer into my mug. "Why so many?"

"China's the top investor in Uganda. Their state-owned companies are doing many infrastructure projects there. Many of their workers start their own businesses in Kampala after their employment contracts are over." Masiko cocks her head sideways. "Why don't you come to Uganda? Earn big money there. I can find you a beautiful contract wife! But you pay me an introduction fee."

My knees suddenly go weak.

2

Mamasans of Pattaya

Soft piano music from loud speakers floats through the air in the nightclub. Clad in a halter-top, a promotional girl strides to a round glass-topped table with Daniel, a *farang*, following behind. She stops a few feet away and motions him to a stool with an open palm. When Daniel is seated, she moves away with a gentle wobble of breasts and a sway of her butt, their cheeks shaped like pomelos.

A flat-chested mamasan appears from a corner of the hall with hair drooping round her sunken cheeks. "Handsome man, I'm Mummy Manee. Welcome." She slides a thick A4-sized menu on the table. "Since now is Happy Hours, it's a buy-one-get-one-free deal – but only for beers." A pair of dark pants is held up around her slim waist by a gem-studded belt, and from her ear lobes dangle a pair of golden earrings attached to tiger's claws.

Daniel scans the menu and looks up at the mamasan. "Chang beer, big." He returns the menu to her who slips it under one armpit. Taking a step backward, she flicks her gaze to a nearby table where three hostesses are stationed. "You see any girls you fancy?"

"Err, no." His eyes are filled with disappointment. "There're not many girls tonight, huh?"

"It's still early and some of my girls are caught in traffic." A smile twists on her crimson lips. "Why don't you ring the bell at the bar counter? Add some excitement to the club! If you need anything, come see me at the back, near the right corner – I am stationed there." She goes away.

Daniel rises from his stool and strides to the bronze bell hanging from a wooden frame next to the bar which runs parallel to the long side of the hall. A sign says "Ring bell if you want to buy drinks for everybody." *Only three bargirls and no patrons in the bar? Well, it won't cost me an arm and a leg.* He pulls the cord attached to the clapper and swings it three times against the soundbow. Three dongs reverberate within the walls of the room. From under the bar, the bartender – a scrawny guy with two canines extending out of his mouth – pulls out a cracker, holds it above his head and pops it! "Yay!" Confetti of fiery red ribbons and chads spray upwards before flustering down.

Six girls strut out through a curtained doorway at the back and head for the bar. Mummy Manee and her promotional girl join them. Two grizzled *farangs* whom Daniel earlier saw hanging outside the front entrance lumber in. "Hooray!" yells one of the cheap Charlies. "He's a jolly good fellow!" Giggles and laughter drift from the lasses gathered at the bar as the bartender preps the drinks.

Thirteen people! That's going to be expensive! A lump forms in Daniel's throat as he returns to his table. *Damn! This is a minor scam!*

* * *

Bouncing bass and a side-winding melody from electronic music rolling out from speakers float like a cloud of dust within the walls of the bar. Sitting with her back facing the wooden counter,

Mummy Tida (not her real name) turns her head to cast a glance at the small red-faced man perched on a high stool beside her. Probably a China-Chinese and in his early twenties, he is taking gentle sips from a tumbler. *What a cheapskate! Not talking with any of my girls and nursing a drink.* Several menus are stacked up on the wooden counter behind her. Like white curls from a gigantic beard, cigarette smoke swirls in the air, blown by cold gusts from air-conditioning vents in the ceiling.

In her early forties, Mummy Tida is wearing a bob hairdo that falls at her collarbone with swept-back side bangs. In spite of a bulbous nose, she is pleasant-looking with an oval face and delicately arched eyebrows. She looks professional in a cream blouse adorned with a golden brooch and dark wide-legged trousers. "Hey, handsome man," she says, turning sideways at her waist, "when you're in a place like this, you must drink like a *real* man."

The Chinese man turns his head sideways. "I don't drink much." A sheepish smile creases his lips as he runs his fingers through his thick black hair. "Back home, I usually drink *baijiu* made from sorghum."

Mummy Tida swivels around on her stool. "Handsome, if you buy me a lady's drink, I'll show you how to drink like a real man!" She rests her splayed hands on the bar. "Deal?" Lights from overhead pendant lamps bounce off the precious gems in the three separate rings of her fingers.

Before the man can reply, Mummy Tida snaps her fingers at the bartender standing behind the counter just a few feet away. "Lady's special!"

From a tray crammed with shot glasses, the bartender slides the lady's drink to Mummy Tida's waiting open palm. "Watch me!" She raises the shot glass to her lips, slams the drink down her throat and glugs it with nary any expression on her face. "Now, you try!"

The man tilts his head backward and upends his tumbler. He scrunches his face and a noisy exhale blasts from his lips. As he replaces the tumbler on the bar with a thud, Mummy Tida reaches out her hand and pats him on one shoulder. "Try again! Practice makes perfect!" *Oh sheesh! With more customers like him, the bar will turn belly up soon!*

She swivels on her bar stool back to her former position and pans the room. The night is still young and only four tables are taken up by patrons and bargirls. In one corner, bargirl Rutna is playing the hammer-the-nail game with a lanky *farang*. Rutna raises the hammer above her shoulder and clobbers the nail smack on its head, driving it into the wooden stump. The *farang* tries but the nail only sinks half way in. "You lose!" Rutna yells. "You buy me another lady's drink!"

Great PR work by Rutna. Strong possibility of her earning a barfine. Mummy Tida swings her attention to the entrance and, within a few minutes, she is rewarded with an athletic-looking *farang* walking in. She slips down from the bar stool, grabs a menu and takes several long strides in leather flats to near the spot where he is standing.

"Hello, sir, welcome!" Crow's feet lines the edges of her eyes as a smile uplifts the corners of her tomato-red lips. *This guy looks distinguished. Slightly bald and has honest eyes. Possibly in his late thirties and in the prime of his career.* "This way, please. I'll escort you to your table." She leads him to a square coffee table with LED strip lighting under the four sides of its top, and he settles down on a plush settee the colour of claret.

Mummy Tida stands with both feet together and holds the menu with both hands. "From where, sir?"

The bug-eyed *farang* hikes his chin and tosses his gaze at her. "Germany." His moustache and goatee make him look like a billy goat.

"Here's the menu, sir." She leans forward and places it in the *farang*'s outstretched hand. "First time in Thailand?" Her gaze darts to the crocodile logo on his blue polo shirt. *Looks like a genuine Lacoste polo shirt.*

The *farang* takes the menu. "Yes, my first night in Pattaya." He opens the menu and casts his gaze down.

"Where are you staying?"

"InterContinental." His gaze flicks up from under blond eyelashes. "Glenlivet, eighteen years." He returns the menu and leans back on the settee. "That's all for the time being."

Wow, an up-market hotel and an expensive bottle! Mummy Tida's smile becomes warmer than the sultry night outside. "An excellent choice of drink, sir." *This is a job for my top girl who charges a premium price, and this farang can bloody afford her.* "Thank you."

Mummy Tida strides to Jintara sitting in an alcove seat a short distance away. The bargirl is garbed in a tight yellow-ochre mini dress that can ignite a ball of fire in any man's groin. Her narrow waist leads down to curvy hips and long shapely legs. "Yes, Mummy?" Her bow-shaped lips open like a lotus blooming and her eyes twinkle like stars.

"*Farang* in blue polo shirt, table six." Mummy Tida's eyes glint with business ruthlessness. "He's loaded! Go for the kill!"

Twenty minutes later, a half-bald man – possibly in his fifties –

wearing flip-flops and khaki cargo shorts lumbers into the club, swaying to the right and then to the left. His t-shirt has the words "I Love Pattaya". Sporting tousled hair and saggy jowls, he looks like he has just woken up.

Mummy Tida, who's been hovering at the side of the entrance, sidles up to him. "*Sawadee-kha!* Welcome!" She studies him through lashes thick with mascara. "May I know where you're from?" *The tan on his face indicates he's been here for a week or more.*

The *farang* peers intently at Mummy Tida, and his breath, smelling of cigarettes and stale whisky, washes over her. "Spain," he says, sputtering saliva, and the next moment, he breaks into a melody, "*Blue Spanish eyes...Teardrops are falling your Spanish eyes...Please, please don't cry* – Engelbert Humperdick's song!"

"Come, follow me." *He's half-drunk and probably has barfined a girl earlier.* She sits him near the stage where the loudspeakers can sometimes be ear-splittingly loud. "Your menu, mister." She passes the menu to his hand and flicks her gaze to his watch strapped around his wrist. "Last call for finger food is an hour's time." *Shucks! It's only a cheap digital watch.*

The *farang* opens the menu, glances at the first page and snaps it shut. "Chang beer, small bottle." He tosses the menu on the coffee table. "Please leave the menu here. I may like to take small bites later." The springs of the chair squeal as he slumps back.

Oh hell! Cheapest beer on the menu! Mummy Tida makes a beeline for Nut who's seated with another co-worker. Endowed with a pockmarked face, Nut is lanky and totally flat-chested. Her canines protruding from beneath her upper lip make her look like a vampire. "Nut! Table eight!" *That fella is only worthy of Nut, my ugliest girl.*

"Part of my job is to assess as many patrons as possible," confesses Mummy Tida after she ends her anecdotes. "If a patron comes in and speaks Thai, my interest in him is lost. That means he's been in Thailand for some time, probably has a Thai girlfriend or even a Thai wife. He knows the market prices and has done it all and seen it all. It's not worth spending too much time and attention on a Pattaya veteran. But, a first-day-and-first-time tourist in Pattaya is like a walking ATM if his wallet is fat. He's more easily excited and is eager to try new things. His clothes, his watch, his aftershave and his hotel are clues to how thick his wallet is. For such patrons, I'll instruct my girls to be extra nice to him, give him a high GFE. Naturally, he gets the pick of my top girls. Top in terms of looks. So, hopefully, he comes back."

I lock gazes with Mummy Tida. "Any funny incidents happened before in this bar?"

"There was this customer who died fucking." A wry smile hovers on Mummy Tida's lips. "He was sixty-two and my bargirl's twenty-six. He barfined her out, took her to a motel. He came and went at the same time."

* * *

"Can I barfine you out?" Michael Kok (not his real name) lifts his gaze from Chintara's deep cleavage to her dark brown eyes. "Make it an exception this time?" She is garbed in a pair of denim hot-pants and a cropped top.

"I've told you before I'm not for barfine and my answer's still no – sorry. I am a coyote dancer." A semblance of a smile flickers on Chintara's lips. "All the bar hostesses can be barfined out." She looks away from his tenacious gaze to several heavily mascared girls seated at a nearby bar table.

Michael leans forward in his bar stool. "I want to barfine you out just for dinner, not sex." He runs a hand over his thick salt-and-pepper hair in a smoothening motion.

"I dance at motor shows, events and clubs – nothing more." She tosses her long hair back. "But I'll be happy to keep you company here for as long as you want me to."

Michael, a fifty-six-year-old Chinese-Malaysian, and Chintara, aged twenty-three, a coyote dancer, are sitting at a round table in Cathy Coyote Bar (name changed). One long side of the hall has a standing bar running parallel to it. On the other side are several curved booths and in the centre is a single column of round bar tables and high stools.

Thirty minutes ago, Chintara and four other dancers were prancing on top of the bar counter. With backs arched, they traced the curves of their hips, thrust their pelvises, pouted their lips and jiggled their breasts. When their dance routine was over, Michael invited her for lady's drinks. Tonight is his fifth visit to Cathy Coyote Bar in a fortnight.

Michael releases an exhale of frustration. "Let me talk to your mamasan."

"Go ahead, but her answer will still be the same." Her silky voice suspends in the air as she casts her gaze down at the empty shot glasses in front of her

"Mummy Natt!" Michael jerks his back straighter, raises one hand and wriggles his fingers. "Yuhoo... Mummy Natt!"

The veteran mamasan – already in her early seventies – sashays over. "Yes? Can I help you?" Her voice is so husky she sounds like a man.

"Mummy, I'd like to barfine Chintara out."

"Sorry, our coyote dancers are showgirls, not bargirls." She shakes her head, causing her dangling earrings to swing. "What's wrong with our hostess girls? They're all playful and fun!" She winks and a deep crow's feet forms at the corner of her eye.

"I'm not interested in them."

A scowl invades Mummy Natt's face, turning it into a mass of wrinkles. "Then you try other coyote bars." She strides away.

Michael tosses his gaze back at Chintara. "How about before work - any day, any time to your convenience."

"Sorry, I don't go out with customers." She slides him a thin smile and looks down at the footrest of the barstool. "Excuse me, I have to go; I've another performance coming up." She perches her stiletto heels on the footrest and climbs down from the bar stool.

Sitting in a lotus position on a woven mat on the floor, *Arjahn* Pulpat, probably in his mid-thirties, leans forward. "What's your problem?" His voice is a mix of harsh and husky.

Wearing a white headgear, he is togged up in a short-sleeved white tunic and white baggy trousers. From a long silver chain around his neck hangs a three-inch pendant in the shape of a black figurine with white fangs.

Gosh! That demonic-looking pendant looks scary. "I want a girl to fall in love with me." Michael expels the words along with shaky air.

Arjahn Pulpat arches his sparse eyebrows. "A Thai girl?"

Michael draws in a calming breath. "Yes."

"How long have you known her?" His small eyes blink as a revolving table fan a few feet away blows swirling smoke from a nearby incense pot towards him.

"Four weeks. I want to marry her."

"I see." *Arjahn* Pulpat nods in understanding. "My first recommendation is a love charm that is for consumption. It is one hundred percent effective but I need the birth particulars of the girl and her full name."

"She's a dancer in a bar and I know her first name." Michael's heart swells with hope. "I should be able to get her date of birth under a false pretext by telling her that I want to give her a present on her birthday."

Arjahn Pulpat clucks his tongue. "Most girls who work in bars don't use their real names." He clasps his hands loosely and rests them between his knees. "You can try to ask her Mummy for her real name but if her mamasan suspects your intention, she won't reveal the information." He wriggles his toes of one foot. "But there is a second option – *num man prai*. This is oil which has been charmed, and you have to anoint it on her. Success rate is also quite high, but it depends on how often you can apply the oil on her – discreetly, of course. The charm will seep through her skin and flow to her heart. She will then become attracted to you."

"Can I pour the oil into a bottle of perfume and give it to her."

"Of course, that'a good idea." *Arjahn* Pulpat unclasps his hands. "So, which method do you prefer?" He straightens up and adjusts his headgear with both hands.

Michael's eyes light up with a sinister glint. "I'll go for the *num mun prai*. You have any in stock now?"

Arjahn Pulpat rises to his feet. "You're lucky. I'll get it for you. It's my last bottle."

Two weeks later...

"Every night, I soak my feet in baking soda dissolved in warm water." Chintara lifts one foot, rests it on one knee and takes off the pointed-toe high-heeled shoe. "See? A bunion is forming on the little toe."

"Oh, you poor thing...Next time when your feet ache, just give me a call." Michael squints to scrutinize her foot under the dim lights. "I can give you a free foot massage." He lifts his gaze upward at her with a smile. "It can be in my place or your place."

Chintara deflects his innuendo by reaching for her glass and slamming the rum down her throat. She looks down at her bare foot, massages her Achilles heel and slips the shoe back.

Michael chugs his beer and plunks the stein down. "By the way, do you like my bottle of perfume?" One corner of his lips quirk in a half smile.

"Yes, very much." Her voice is hollow, like a shell.

"Have you been using it?"

"A little."

Michael clears his throat. "Err, how about going out with me after work tonight?"

"Sorry, I've a headache. In fact I'm planning to leave early."

Sheesh! Maybe she's not using enough of the perfume. "In that case, I better call it a night too. Thank you so much for your company." *Hmmm...Maybe Arjahn Pulpat's charm doesn't work.* Michael looks around for the mamasan and spots her. *Anyway, let's see what happens next week.* "Yuhooo...Mummy!" He raises one arm and makes a scribbling motion with his thumb and forefinger held together. "My bill, please."

When the bill is paid, Mummy Natt, togged up in a beige pantsuit, walks in step with Michael to accompany him to the door. Outside, standing on the pavement, she latches her knobby hand on his wrist for a moment. "Michael, thank you for coming." A twisted toothy smile forms on her scrawny face which looks like that of an embalmed corpse. "I really appreciate your regular business over the past several weeks. As a token of appreciation, can I buy you a late supper? I know an excellent Italian restaurant that's within walking distance." She raises one hand to finger the strands of her bob hair at one side. "I can leave the bar now if you're kind enough to accept my invitation."

Mummy Natt cuts the tom yum pizza set in the centre of the table into two pieces and puts the knife down. Using a fork and a spoon she transfers one half to Michael's plate. "There you are – be careful, it's hot." She takes the remaining half and picks up her fork and knife. "You must be an interesting person. Can you tell me more about yourself?" She starts to cut her pizza into bite sizes. "Which part of Malaysia are you from?"

"I'm from Penang, just retired last year." Michael unfolds his napkin and puts it on his lap. "I've decided to make Pattaya my new home. I love the food, the beaches and the nightlife." He starts to eat. "Maybe I'll start a self-service launderette later."

When Michael and Mummy Natt have partaken of the pizza, they start to sip their drinks and make small talk. Partway, Mummy slides her chair closer to the table and Michael feels something moving against his crotch. He looks down and his eyes span wider in shock. *Sweet suffering saints!* One bare foot of Mummy Natt is twiddling its toes against his crotch! Heat simmers from his fingertips up to his arms and spreads into his cheeks. He slides his chair backward with a screech.

Mummy Natt locks her gaze on Michael with twinkling eyes.

"Shall we go to a love motel after this?" The twinkle in her eyes glints with lust. "I don't mind paying for the room." Her ruby-red lips curve into a sly smile. "I've strawberry-flavoured condoms in my handbag."

"What!" Michael blanches and his dickie shrivels. "Err, I've got an early appointment tomorrow. I've gotta go after this!" He starts to wolf down his pizza.

Back to the present...

"After my date with Michael, I knew I was not my usual self because I always maintain a professional relationship with my customers." Mummy Natt takes a drag of her cigarette, causing her cheeks to sink inward. "I suspected the cause was black magic and I was able to pinpoint it to the perfume that Chintara gave to me." She protrudes her lower lip to blow smoke upward. "That charmed perfume was given to her by Michael. I later went for a cleansing ritual in a temple."

"And why did Chintara give it to you?" I take a sip of my champagne cocktail and continue to hold the fluted glass in my hand.

"Chintara said she had too many bottles already. She also didn't quite like the fragrance. At first, she didn't mention that it came from Michael but only revealed it when I questioned her." She leans forward on the table to tap ash on a Johnnie Walker ashtray, and a hint of cleavage peeks out the neckline of her dress. "Then I told her about the effects of Michael's perfume on me. I also advised her to be careful of her shoes – don't let them fall into Michael's possession or that of any other man."

"Huh? Shoes?" I draw my eyebrows together in question. "How do you mean?"

Mummy Natt narrows her eyes with the intensity of one sharing a secret. "*Num mum prai* can also work if it is smudged on the victim's shoes. For example, assume your live-in girlfriend has left you but she has left behind a pair of old shoes. Apply *num mum prai* on her old shoes and the black magic can still work."

"Holy cow! That's scary." I twirl the stem of the fluted glass between my thumb and forefinger and look around me. As it is still early, only four customers are in the coyote bar. I put the fluted glass on the table and rise to my feet. "Mummy, as a token of appreciation for your time spent talking with me, I'm going to ring the bell." I point at my chit bin. "Prepare my bill, please."

Mummy Natt rewards me with a twisted toothy smile.

When I return to my table, Mummy Natt looks up from perusing my bill. "Before you leave, let me tell you a joke." She puts the bill on the silver platter set in front of me. "You've seen that sign 'Good Guys Go to Heaven; Bad Guys Go to Pattaya' isn't it?" Mummy pauses. "Now, there's this young macho *farang* who dies in a scooter accident in Pattaya and meets St. Peter. St.Peter asks him whether he has been a bad guy or a good guy? The *farang* says he has been bad and wants to go back to Pattaya. St. Peter says his wish is granted." Mummy twirls her hands and stretches out her manicured fingers. "Alakazam! The *farang* finds himself on Walking Street. He is delighted but feels strange. He runs his hands over his chest and his crotch. Oh Lord Buddha, he has been sent back to Pattaya as a Thai ladyboy!"

* * *

I step inside Stalingrad Bar (not its real name) and an usherette directs a hand to a round table draped with a white cloth at one corner. Layers of percussive thunks are bouncing off the walls of the hall to the beats of electronic squelches from a synthesizer. I grab a seat and a statuesque Russian hostess sashays to my table with a wiggle of hips on her stilettos. "Hello, darling! I'm Nikita!" she says, sitting beside me. "I'm from Moscow. You from Taiwan?" Before I can respond, a waitress sets a tumbler glass in front of Nikita and drops a chit in the metal bin which looks like a pencil holder.

Up next is the stocky mamasan who has a heavy and ill-natured face. She sets a menu in front of me, says "Nikita will take care of you" and goes away.

Earlier, while I was sauntering past the entrance of Stalingrad Bar, two blond bombshells, wrapped in tight sequined sheath dresses, cajoled me with, "Russian girls inside! Pole dancing upstairs!" I fell for the bait.

Presently, I refocus my attention on Nikita – whose face look like a Barbie doll's – and say, "I'm from Shanghai, China."

Nikita extends her hand and I pump it. "Ah... Russia and China are allies, almost like sweethearts!" She forms a heart with the thumbs and forefingers of both hands and smiles to reveal dimples and perfect teeth. "You like Russian girls?"

I dip my hand inside the bin, take out the chit and look at the figure. Great balls of fire! Five hundred baht for a lady's drink. That's almost three times the prices at regular bars. Ditto for prices in the menu when I read it. A lump forms in my throat.

"Excuse me, I wanna go upstairs to watch the dancing." I rise, weave through gaps between tables and climb up the staircase to the first floor. Holding my bin in one hand and her lady's drink in another, Nikita follows behind and we take a table near a small stage with a chrome pole where a lithe blonde is contorting herself around it.

The moment Nikita puts the bin on our table, a waitress drops a chit inside. I pick it up and look at it. One thousand baht as cover charge to watch the show! As I return the chit into the bin, Nikita empties her glass and orders another lady's drink.

Fifteen minutes pass as Nikita and I talk about nightclubs and stripper clubs in Moscow and I ask for my bill before she can order a third lady's drink.

"Leaving so soon?" asks the mamasan putting the black bill folder on my table. "Why? You don't like my girls?"

I take out my wallet. "Prices here are expensive." I count some money notes and toss them on the bill folder.

"What? You cannot afford our prices? Then, you fuck off! Get lost!" The spark in the mamasan's eyes matches the fire I feel in my gut.

Outside, I pass an adjacent bar and a Thai pamphlet girl wearing triangular earrings steps up to me. "Handsome man, I saw you go inside and come out quickly. It's expensive huh? Russian bars in Pattaya have hot Russian girls but at hot prices." Her broad face contracts with a grimace. "Too hot for many men for handle." She directs an open palm at the entrance of her bar. "Why not come to our bar? We've hot Thai girls, but at cool prices!"

*　*　*

The moto-taxi driver, nearing fifty in age, grabs the front panels of his reflective yellow vest and squares his shoulders. "No, I don't know any ping-pong show performer. But I know a *former* ping-pong show performer! She's now working as a mamasan in an ago-go bar." He folds his arms across his chest. "If you buy her lady's drinks, give her a big tip, she can tell you stories about herself." He unfolds his arms, drops them at his sides. "You want to meet her? I can take you to her bar now."

"Okay, but where are we going?"

"Magic Waves Go-Go Bar (name changed)."

"Your fare?"

"According to the standard rates fixed by our Ministry of Transport. But you pay me a tip of two hundred baht for introducing the mamasan to you. Deal?"

"Deal."

The moto-taxi driver moves to his moped which is parked a few feet away, opens the back carrier and takes out a German-style open-face helmet. "Wear this helmet, please." He kicks at the starter and its engine sputters to life. "Come on, climb aboard." He gets on the moped, kicks its side stand up and I climb up behind him. We chug into traffic with the moped popping and sputtering.

Fifteen minutes later, after weaving in and out of lines of vehicles, we stop outside Magic Waves Go-Go Bar which has a woven-acrylic-fibre awning protruding over its sidewalk. The moped stops in front of the pavement with a squeal of brakes and I get off. The driver dismounts, leans the moped on its side stand and strides towards the bar.

Inside, there is no one at the reception desk in the small foyer, indicating we are very early. At the end of the foyer, the moto-taxi driver pushes a thick cretonne curtain aside and we enter a hall furnished with round tables and steel dining chairs. A sweeping curved steel staircase with wrought iron balusters leads to the first floor. Two bargirls are seated at a table. One of them, a petite girl wearing tinted blond shoulder-length hair, has one foot resting on the edge of her chair, and she is applying varnish on her toe nails. Her co-worker, her hair tied up in a pony tail, is fiddling with her mobile phone.

The moto-taxi driver walks to the bargirls and stops a few feet away from their table. "*Mamasan Lamai xyu thihin?*"

The fake blonde looks up for a second and focuses her attention back to her task, while the ponytailed girl gets up from her chair and clomps on wedges into the back entranceway at the far end of the hall.

The moto-taxi driver goes to sit at an adjacent table. "Come, mister," he says to me, "sit down." I pull a steel chair out and settle down. Moments later, the ponytailed girl reappears with the mamasan – probably late twenties, of average height and slightly overweight – wearing bob hairstyle and faux-leather ankle boots.

The ponytailed girl returns to her former spot and the mamasan comes to our table and takes a seat. She has on a black maxi skirt and creamy beige shirt dress with two unbuttons undone, showing lots of cleavage, with nipples protruding subtly through the fabric.

The moto-taxi driver and the mamasan say something to each other in Thai language and she flicks her gaze to me and back to the moto-taxi driver. A gentle smile tugs at the corners of her lips and she swings her gaze back to me. "Hello! I am Mummy Lamai!" Leaning forward, she extends her hand, her wrist adorned with a fat gold bracelet.

"What's your name?"

"Jackson," I lie. "Please let me buy you as many lady's drinks as you want."

Mummy Lamai casts her gaze at the bartender standing

behind the counter a few feet away and hollers, "Two lady's drink!" She pauses. "Ratana, bring the menu here." She returns her gaze to me. "So, what do you want to know?"

"Your experiences as a ping-pong show performer."

The ponytailed girl hands me a two-page menu and waits for my order. I flip to the back which lists a variety of beers. "Singha beer."

Before I can return the menu, the moto-taxi driver swipes it away and, after giving it a cursory glance, says to the ponytailed girl, "Buffalo wings, spring rolls, Chang beer, big bottle!" He returns the menu to her, then tosses his gaze at me and grins. "While both of you talk, I'll keep busy by eating."

A smile plays on Mummy Lamai's lips and as she starts to play raconteur, I gaze into her past mentally...

Six years ago...
Mongkut, the grizzled headman of Samakhi village, Roi Et Province, flits his gaze across the faces of the six members of his Bung Fai Festival Celebration Committee. They are sitting across him on a plaited reed mat in his living room, where an overhead ceiling fan is groaning as it swirls warm afternoon air around.

Mongkut takes a sip of his *oliang*, puts the glass down on the reed mat and sits straighter. "My fellow villagers, harvest has been moderate last season so we've limited funds for the Bung Fai Festival. To make things worse, our previous sponsor has backed out because of budget constraints." He draws in a deep breath as if to bolster himself. "Our village will lose face if we do not have a presence in the festival. Therefore, we have to participate but in cost-effective ways. Anybody has any suggestion?"

Celebrated annually before the paddy-planting season in

the Isaan provinces, the Bung Fai Festival features dances, float parades and merry-making. Rockets are launched to remind the sky god Phaya Taen to send his rain for the paddy crops. Phallic symbols are displayed to invoke fertility for the crops so that there will be a bountiful harvest.

A scrawny man with a weather-beaten face raises one calloused hand for a moment. "Sir, we can recycle last year's costumes and put up a dance performance during the parade. But for this year, our dancers will perform on top of a decorated cart drawn by water buffalos! The water buffalos will be dressed up, of course."

"Excellent idea!"

"Sir," says Kittibun, Lamai's father, "I can build a rocket if you can give me the funds to buy the ingredients. Hopefully, it will win a prize this year."

Mongkut raises his grey eyebrows. "You sure, you know how to do it?"

"Yes, a friend can teach me the process. Instead of using a PVC pipe, I can use bamboo which is free. Vines from creepers can replace steel wires to cut costs further."

"How big will your bamboo rocket be?"

"That will depend on the quantities of the three ingredients – sulphur, potassium citrate and black carbon – that we can afford to buy. I can give you quotations tomorrow."

"Great!" The corners of Mongkut's lips tip up. "I'll get a few volunteers to search for the fattest possible bamboo!"

Suwannaphum, three weeks later....
Under a scorching afternoon sun, at the far end of a football field, stands a stage for singing and dance performances in the evening.

Hordes of spectators are milling around and food stalls under tents are doing brisk trade. A row of launch pads constructed of bamboo poles are standing in a line parallel to the length of the field. Resembling step ladders, they rise from twenty to thirty feet high. Leaning against one side of the respective launch pads are rockets of various sizes.

Mongkut, members of his Bung Fai Festival Celebration Committee and dozens of fellow villagers are gathered several feet away from a giant rocket made by Kittibun. Thus far, four rockets have been launched by other participants, and the panel of judges has evaluated their performances in terms of height achieved and beauty of vapour trials.

Soon, a voice from a loud hailer in the judges' tent announces, "Next participant is Samakhi Village! Please launch your rocket now!"

Mongkut says to Kittibun, "The honour is yours, Kittibun! After all, you single-handedly made this rocket!"

"Yay!" holler the other members of the committee. "Go, Kittibun! Go! Go! Go!" They take several steps backward from the rocket, their faces grinning with delight.

"Thank you, sir." Togged up in a short-sleeved shirt, Kittibun steps forward to the bamboo rocket, then pulls out a cigarette lighter from his shirt pocket and snaps it open. He holds his hand high up to bring the cigarette-lighter flame to the fuse. Nothing happens. He continues to hold the flame to the fuse. The fuse suddenly burns with the speed of lightning! In the next instant, the bamboo rocket explodes with a deafening boom! Mongkut and his entourage scream in horror and instinctively crouch to the ground. White smoke wafts around them for several seconds.

"Arrrrrrgh!" Kittibun writhes on the ground, his face

scrunched in agony, his clothes covered with blood, and his left hand clutches at his right upper arm.

As the smoke starts to drift away, Mongkut rushes to where Kittibun lay sprawled and the former's chin drops. "Oh Lord Buddha! His lower right arm has been blown away!" He hollers to his fellow villagers, "Let's get him to the hospital!"

That same evening, Mrs. Kittibun says to her twenty-one-year-old daughter during dinner, "Lamai, not only has your father lost an arm but his right leg was also seriously injured. The hospital doctor says he will have to use crutches to walk for the rest of his life." A sad sigh shudders from her lips. "I'm afraid we cannot remain in this farm any more. I'll be going to Roi Et town in a few days' time to look for work."

"I understand, *Mae* [Mum]." Lamai's throat convulses with a hard swallow. "I will go to Pattaya to work." Unwanted moisture starts to mist her eyes.

Pattaya, six months later...
Three bargirls in the small dressing room of Pink Parrot Bar (not its real name) are in various stages of undress as they are changing into their work clothes. Lamai and another co-worker are sitting at a dresser each, applying make-up. A tattoo sounds on the door which swings open and the mamasan – donned in black sequin-embellished pants and red, shiny heels – steps inside.

In the dresser mirror facing Lamai, Mummy sees the reflection of a plump dark-skinned girl wearing short hair with a side parting. Her broad nose that is too big for her round face is set above a wide mouth, and her sole attractive feature is the long curly eyelashes that give life to her big brown eyes.

"Lamai," says the mamasan, "can you come to my room

after you've finished?"

"Yes, Mummy."

Minutes later, Lamai is sitting facing Mummy in her cubicle where several shelves are stuffed with party hats, Haloween masks and Santarina costumes.

"Lamai, I'm disappointed with your performance." Mummy rests her elbows on her desk and leans forward. "You've been inconsistent in meeting your quotas on lady's drink and barfines." She looks down at a black book in front of her. "For last month and the previous month, you've missed your quotas. This is now the middle of June. So far, your figures have been disappointing and I doubt you can hit the quota for this month." She closes the book with a snap and pushes it aside. "You've to buck up or I will have no choice but to let you go." Her eyes blaze with fire. "Now, what's your problem in meeting quotas?"

"Err, I guess I'm not pretty enough."

"Then, slim down and go for plastic surgery!" The tone of her voice is as mean as the scowl on her face.

Standing on the pavement of an alley, a tout, probably in his mid-twenties, accosts a passing pot-bellied *farang* togged up in shorts and a t-shirt. "Ping-pong show, sir! Ping-pong show!" He shoves a piece of laminated paper towards the *farang* whose flip-flops are slapping loudly on the concrete.

The *farang* swings a fleeting gaze at the tout. "No, thank you!" He begins to take longer and faster steps away from the tout.

From a short distance away under the lights of a lamp post, Lamai, garbed in a t-shirt and blue jeans, has been observing the tout. Now she approaches him and stops a few feet away. "Where can I find your boss? I want to talk with him."

The tout's brows inch up in surprise. "Why?"

"I want to work for him."

The tout turns sideways at the hip and points to his left. "See that staircase door? The one with a string of coloured bulbs above. Go up and ask for Mr. Khemkhaeng."

"Thank you." Lamai turns on her heels and walks in the direction as shown.

Moments later, she pushes aside a thick heavy curtain at the staircase landing and enters a hall filled with several rows of chairs. At the end of the hall is a small stage with a drum set standing at one side.

A jimber-jawed man sitting at a table just inside the door entrance rises to his feet. "Miss, what do you want?" The cigarette on his lip dances as he speaks

"I'm looking for Mr. Khemkhaeng."

"I'm Khemkhaeng. How can I help you?" In his forties, he has thick eyebrows and tattoos on his neck.

"I want to work as a ping-pong show performer." Lamai's friendly expression fades to serious. "I've no experience but I'm willing to learn."

"Come and see me tomorrow at 11 a.m." He takes out a name card. "The door will be locked but I'll be here, so give me a call when you arrive."

The next morning, Lamai and Khemkhaeng come out of the latter's cubicle as three women are doing kegal exercises on the stage. They squat and stand repeatedly, bawling in unison, "Tighten!... Squat!...Up!...Release!.. Tighten!... Squat!...Up!... Release!.. Tighten!... Squat!...Up!...Release!"

With Lamai in tow, Khemkhaeng climbs up the wooden steps to the stage and claps his hands. "Attention, ladies! Sorry to interrupt your warm-up."

Togged up in black yoga leotards, the three women exhale and look at Lamai with curious eyes.

Khemkhaeng directs an arm at his recruit. "Ladies, this is Lamai. She will join us as an apprentice starting tomorrow." He snaps his gaze at a woman with a square face and thick eyebrows. "Siriporn, please train her as best as you can. I want Lamai to perform in a supporting role in two weeks' time and as a star in the second month!" Khemkhaeng pats Lamai on the shoulder with a gnarled hand. "Alright, you're now in Siriporn's good hands." He turns and leaves the stage.

Siriporn steps closer to Lamai. "Welcome aboard! Now, Lamai, the first thing you need is to buy a set of weighted vaginal cones."

"Huh?" Lamai squishes her brows. "What's that?"

"I'll show you." Siriporn moves to one of three sports bags lying at one end of the stage, unzips it open and takes out a small plastic container about the size of a hand-held calculator. She returns to her former spot, holds the container in the palm of her hand and opens the lid. Inside are four shiny metal weights of different sizes in the shape of rings and a small plastic cone with a length of cord at one end.

"How do I use this?"

"Hold this." Siriporn hands the container to Lamai.

From the container, Siriporn takes out the cone and begins to turns one half in an anti-clockwise direction. "Unscrew the cone, insert a weight in the spindle" – she picks up a metal ring and slips it on the spindle – "and screw the two halves back."

She starts to go through the motion of inserting a tampon. "Insert the cone into your vagina and tighten your pelvic floor muscles. Hold the weighted cone for fifteen minutes, three times a day, while you're doing light household chores. As your muscles get stronger, increase the weight." Siriporn replaces the cone in its container and takes it back from Lamai. "You can buy this set from a pharmacy. Your training begins tomorrow at 11 a.m. Bring your set along."

A month later...

With his back facing the stage at one end, Aroon, the thirty-something-year-old bouncer, scans the audience. *I hope no one tries to climb up to the stage tonight!*

Standing in the left wing of the stage, the emcee announces, "Ladieees and jeeentlemen! Our first performer is Miss Lamai, Pattaya's Pussy of Iron! Please give her a good hand!"

A drum roll sounds and ends with a crash of cymbals. Overhead lights brighten the stage. The garish curtain parts and Lamai, garbed in a glittery robe strides in heels to centre-stage and takes a bow to the applause of the audience. With a flourish, she takes off her robe to reveal a black sequin bustier top wrapped around her upper torso but a naked lower torso. Her right thigh has a tattoo of a cowboy-style revolver which is wrapped by a bowtie garter belt. On her left thigh is a tattoo of a garter belt.

Aroon flicks a momentary gaze at Lamai. *The more I look at the tattoos, the more I like them. She's damn creative!* He returns his attention to the audience who comprise foreign male tourists and a few couples. *So far so good, there's no one holding up a camera to do video-recording.*

To the accompaniment of *chck, chck, chck, chck, chck* sounds created by the drummer closing the hi-hat cymbals repeatedly, Lamai moves an upholstered bench to the apron of the stage, one end facing the audience. She lies down and raises her legs high in the air and spreads them. "Ooooohh! Nice pussy!" hollers a silver-haired man – hunched from age – sitting in the front row, wiping saliva trickling from his mouth with a spotless white handkerchief.

From the left wing, a female assistant appears with a square wire cage containing what look like several live frogs. The assistant moves to Lamai's right side, opens the top lid of the container and Lamai dips her hand inside and picks up a big bullfrog. She holds the amphibian high up for a moment for the audience to see. A drum roll starts as Lamai starts to insert the frog inside her genitals. The drummer taps the tom-tom drum. *Tok!* Then he crashes the cymbals. *Chiaaang!* Lamai raises her arms, each of her hands forming a "V" sign. "Haaaaaaiyaah!" The frog has disappeared inside her girl-parts! The assistant passes a microphone to Lamai which holds it to her groin. Raucous croaking blasts from speakers at the sides of the stage.

"Is the frog real?" asks the emcee.

The audience goes batshit, yelling, "Yeeeeeees!" A few men stand up to get a better look.

Suddenly, a young Asian man, his face flushed from alcohol, his forehead covered with hair fallen from the top of his head, leaps from his middle end seat on the fourth row and starts hopping like a frog on the floor in the middle aisle. "I'm a frog! Croak! Croak! Croak!" Face wreathed with a big grin, he starts to head in the direction of the stage. "I'm a frog! Put me inside your pussy!"

While the Asian man's friends laugh uproariously, Aroon

strides to the middle aisle and hustles the man away. "Go back to your seat, sir! Please go back!"

Lamai's performance ends after several more erotic acts, and the show continues with other performers.

A year later...

On this particular night, the ping-pong show theatre is a full house. At the tail end of Lamai's act, the emcee announces, "Now for her finale, Miss Lamai will perform the dangerous pussy-eat-razor blade act!"

Earlier, Lamai performed the "pussy-write-letter", "pussy-cut-banana" and "pussy-smoke-cigarette" acts. Having been in "show-biz" for almost a year, the "pussy-eat-razor" act is routine for her as she has done it dozens of times.

A smile plastered on her face, Lamai takes a bow and, from inside her bustier, produces several razor blades held together with a nylon string. She unfurls the nylon string and pulls it taut to reveal six razor blades tied at regular intervals. They glint menacingly under the bright lights. A female assistant steps out from the right wing holding six balloons on sticks in one hand and moves to arm's length from Lamai.

"Ladies and gentlemen," says the hidden emcee, "as you will see, the razor blades are real!"

Lamai holds the first razor in the row and cuts a balloon. *Pop!* She repeats the task with the other razor blades consecutively, popping the other five balloons, and the assistant goes away. Now, she bunches the razors together and holds them high in one hand for a moment. Then, she lies down on the upholstered bench and spreads her legs wide.

As Lamai starts to insert the razor blades inside her girl-parts, the drummer starts a buzz roll on the snare drum. A few tense moments pass. Voila! The razor blades have slid inside, leaving a short length of nylon string outside her body, and the drummer clobbers the cymbals – *chiaaang!* – while Lamai raises both hands, two fingers of each hand forming a V-sign. Amidst loud applause, Lamai rolls sideways off the bench and stands. To the staccato beat of drums, she gyrates, thrusts her pelvis repeatedly and performs upper body undulations. She returns to the upholstered bench, lies down and raises her legs high once again. The drummer starts a buzz roll, and with her forefingers and thumbs, Lamai starts to pulls one end of the nylon string away to draw the razor blades out.

When the second razor blade appears, the ceiling lights come on. A hoarse voice hollers, "Run! Run! Police! Police! Run!" The next moment, several policemen try to barge into the hall as Khemkhaeng's tout, ticket-seller and usherette form a barricade at the entrance door. Aroon, stationed at his usual place near the stage, springs into action. *Dammit! I gotta delay the cops so that our girls have time to flee.* He dashes to join the trio jostling with the policemen.

Meanwhile, the drummer throws his drum sticks away, leaps off his stool and runs to the left wing. The emcee hitherto standing in the left wing has already fled, leaving his microphone behind on the floor! The drummer bolts to the back door where there is a ladder leading down to the back lane.

Lamai scuttles like a crab with legs straddled towards the left wing. Halfway, she falls and lets out an agonizing scream. She tries to get up, blood flowing down the insides of her thighs. "Arrrrrrrgh!" Face contorted in pain, she sinks to her knees and falls on her butt, her legs spread apart, blood dripping from her girl-parts. Aroon casts a quick gaze at the stage and sees Khemkhaeng bolting past Lamai, who's still struggling to get to her feet. *Oh Lord Buddha! Lamai has been cut!* Aroon rushes up the stage and dashes to where Lamai is sitting. "I'll carry you piggy back!" He turns his back towards her and squats. Lamai mounts his back and Aroon supports her legs and lifts her up. Together, they lumber to the left wing and escape through the back door.

Aroon places a comforting hand on Lamai's. "How are you feeling?" His nostrils twitch as the smell of disinfectant assails them.

Lying on a hospital bed, Lamai shifts her head in her pillow. "The bleeding has stopped but the wounds are still painful." She bites her lower lip. "Aroon, I want to check out by today. I can't afford to stay here longer."

"But without medical care, the wound may get infected. Tell you what, I'll subsidize half of your medical costs. That's the best I can do."

Lamai squeezes Aroon's hand. "Thank you so much."

Back to the present...

"That was my worst experience as a ping-pong show dancer." Mummy Lamai takes a glug of her lady's drink, upending the glass. "It has left me traumatized and I became too scared to perform again." An exhale blasts from her lips. "So, I became a coyote dancer for several years before ending up as a mamasan here." She gently puts the glass back on the table.

As a man walks past our table, he turns his head to say something to Mummy Lama who replies in the same language.

She returns her attention to me. "That's Aroon, my husband. He's the head bouncer here." Her gaze drops to my empty beer bottle. "Another Singha beer?"

I nod. She gives a hand signal to the bartender and we chat about her early life in Isaan.

The ponytailed bimbo deposits my bottle of Singha beer in front of me.

Eyes gleaming, Mummy Lamai gazes at the bottle which is unopened. "I still miss the applause of the audience." With a mischievous grin on her lips, she reaches out and grabs my bottle. "Can I borrow your handkerchief?"

"Of course." I tug out my folded handkerchief from my shirt pocket and hand it to her who wraps the bottle cap with it.

Mummy rises from her chair. "Come let's go behind the bar. Let me show you the pussy-open-bottle act." She trots towards the bar and I follow her.

Behind the bar, Mummy hollers to the bartender standing nearby, "Arthit, just continue working and don't look at me, okay?" She flicks her gaze at me. "Jackson, are you ready?"

I nod.

Mummy kneels on the floor, pulls the hem of her skirt higher and shoves the beer bottle between her legs. "Uggh!" Face scrunching with effort, she squirms her lower torso, blasting out noisy exhales. "Argh...uggh!" Seconds later, she pulls out the beer bottle, unwraps the handkerchief and returns it to me. The bottle cap has been prised off! It drops to the floor. "Yay, I can still do it!" She gets up and passes the bottle to me. "Now, drink your beer from the bottle!" A little-girl giggle erupts from her lips.

Taking the bottle, I smile sheepishly, scan the hall and spot a fat balding *farang* with an empty mug in front of him. I round the bar and walk up to the roly-poly.

"Hey, buddy, have a bottle of beer on me!" I put the beer bottle on his table.

"Cheers!" He grabs the bottle, brings it his lips and drinks copiously. "Thank you, mate!"

3

Suicide Capital
of Southeast Asia

The tropical sun shines fiercely on the cluster of houses in a small village in Sompoi district in Chaiyaphum Province, four hours by bus from Bangkok. In the living room of one of these houses sit twenty-eight-year-old Shane, who hails from Europe, his girlfriend Wanicha, aged twenty-four, her father Anurak and her mother on a plaited straw mat spread on the floor.

In front of them are platters of *kluay tod* (banana fritters) and *poh pia tod* (spring rolls). The four people are nibbling the snacks, sipping iced tea and making small talk. When the snacks have been consumed, Anurak segues to the purpose of the meeting. "So, Shane, I heard that you and Wanicha are making future plans?" His English is heavily accented.

Shane nods. "Yes, sir, I wish to marry Wanicha." He is dressed in a spotless white cotton t-shirt and khaki cargo pants.

Anurak assesses Shane through lustreless eyes. "What are you working as?"

"I'm a packaging supervisor in a beer factory."

Wanicha adds, "It's a big factory." She has a broad face and a wide nose. Her thick lips are pushed together to form a small mouth.

"What do you plan to do in Pattaya?"

"Teach English. To supplement my income I'll be a part-time real estate agent."

"Have you ever been married?"

"No, sir."

"How much *sinsod* are you prepared to pay?"

"Perhaps it's better that you suggest a figure."

A wry smile flickers on Anurak's lips. "If I suggest, it will be a big figure. So it is better that you give me a figure to start the ball rolling."

"Err, how about fifty thousand?"

"What!" Smirking, Anurak clutches his chest in a mock heart attack. "So little?"

Wanicha shoots her father a mortified look. "*Phx*, this is not the time for jokes."

Shane stares a split second at Anurak in embarrassment and the latter's face breaks out in a smile. "Sorry for the joke, Shane." His smile quickly disappears. "To be frank, we are not after your money but too little *sinsod* will make us lose face in the eyes of our relatives. Also, behind your back, they will call you a *farang xu nk* – that's a common Thai expression. It means bird-shit foreigner. You understand? So can you do better than fifty thousand?"

"Yes, I've a Plan B." He sucks in an inhale. "Here's what I suggest." He releases a noisy exhale. "I will not only pay the *sinsod* of fifty thousand but I'll also pay a stipend of five thousand baht every month to you for six months. Of course, later on, I'll help out as and when necessary."

Anurak arches his eyebrows. "Stipend?"

"An allowance, to put it in a simple term."

Anurak drifts his gaze to his wife and they say something in

Thai language to each other. He looks back at Shane. "Six months for err, – how to say? – stipend is too short a period. You've also missed my point of us not losing face." He pauses for emphasis. "So…we propose a *sinsod* of one hundred thousand baht but, in private, we'll return fifty thousand to you. But the payment of stipend will be for one year, not six months. How does that sound to you?"

Wanicha's lips tip up in a happy smile. "That's a great idea, *Phx*!" She flicks her gaze to Shane. "Oh, darling, then you won't be called a bird-shit foreigner behind your back!"

"Yes, sir, I agree. It's a win-win situation."

One month later…

Shane swallows a few bites of his fried spring roll. "Darling, I saw an online ad on a cheap apartment for rent." He takes a quick swig of his pineapple juice. "Maybe we can go check it out tomorrow?"

"Sorry Shane, I'm not interested." Wanicha's eyes flick up from the plate of *pad Thai* noodles in front of her to meet his, tugging a sigh from her lips. "In fact, I've something important to tell you." She crimps her brows. "It's very difficult for me to say it but…"

Shane and Wanicha are sitting in the patio of a sea-facing café on Jomtien Beach, five kilometres south of Pattaya. Above, the sun's rays are thrusting its shafts of light through gaps in the soufflé of gray clouds forming in the distance.

Shane's fuzzy brows lift in question. "What's so difficult to talk about to your friend and soulmate and future husband?"

Wanicha sucks in a deep breath as if to draw in courage. "I want to cancel our marriage." The tone of her voice is dry.

"What!" Shane's body goes stiff, with heat searing his cheeks. "Is this some kind of a joke?" He locks gazes with Wanicha.

She puts down her fork and spoon on the table. "No, Shane, I'm serious."

The beating of Shane's heart pulses in his ears. "But why?"

"Because you're not rich enough." She stares at him with sober eyes. "Another *farang* has proposed to me. He owns a big business in California, drives a big car back home and has promised to buy a luxury condo for me." Hardness is etched on her face. "He can give me a better life than you."

Shane's shoulders sag. "How long have you known him?"

"I met him months before I resigned from the bar, but we've been in touch by email and Skype."

He slumps in his chair. "You sure you want to marry him?"

"Yes, Shane, I'm sure."

"Say it again to my face."

Wanicha fuses her gaze to his. "Yes, I'm sure." The resolve in her voice lances his heart.

"I should have known!" He spits the words out through clenched teeth. "You bargirls are only after money! I thought you're different from the rest, but I was wrong." Looking beyond Wanicha, he raises one hand. "Waiter, my bill, please." His vision begins to blur from tears. "I'm going back to my hotel now. You can take a separate tuk-tuk back."

Two days later...

A timid young security guard at Mesong Garden Inn (not its real name), casts his gaze at the drag beyond the front entrance of the hotel. Vehicle traffic is minimal as it's after midnight and the street lamps are alternately casting shadows and bathing the pavement in yellow hues. It's time for him to make a patrol around the perimeter walkway of the hotel. He takes out an amulet from his pocket and utters to himself, "Oh Lord Buddha, protect me from evil spirits." From the front porch, he starts to walk towards the back yard which serves as a parking lot. Partway down the side alley, something falls from above onto the ground with a loud thud. The security guard jumps in shock. Sweating all over, he goes to the spot where a body is lying. In the semi-darkness he makes out a *farang* sprawled in a pool of blood. *Oh Lord Buddha! One of our guests has committed suicide. He must have jumped from a balcony.*

Another three days later...

Little raindrops pitter-patter on the umbrellas of pedestrians sauntering on the streets of Pattaya, and gentle breezes seem to whisper a sad tune. Inside the hall of a temple, a white coffin with brass handles is displayed together with a framed photo of the deceased on a separate table choked with flowers. From the photo, Shane is smiling a boyish smile, with a twinkle in his blue eyes. Four monks garbed in saffron robes are standing beside the coffin and chanting prayers which echo eerily in the hall: "*Phraphuth thcea xngkh nhung, xwyphr cit dwng wiyyan khn ni hi klabklay pen mnusy thi sungsng...*"

Ten feet away, Shane's father Patrick, his mother and twenty-something younger sister are standing facing the coffin. They are wearing dark clothes and Shane's mother, a portly woman, has a pair of shades wrapped around her eyes. A lean man with a long face and sunken cheeks, Patrick is muttering to himself, "Shane, you've died too young...Oh Lord, please forgive me...Dear God, how can I ever forgive myself?"

Wanicha is kneeling on the floor next to Shane's sister. Shane's face in the photograph is floating before Wanicha in a wash of tears. She has on a white blouse and dark pants. Among the others present are four bargirls from the ago-ago club where Wanicha once worked. Partway through the ceremony, Patrick's head droops, his eyes roll upward and he crumples on the floor in a heap.

Shane's sister yells, "Oh my God, Daddy has fainted!"

The four bargirls spring to their feet and rush towards Patrick's prone body. One of them points to several wooden benches lined against one wall and hollers to Wanicha, "Put three benches side by side together! We'll put him on top!"

Wanicha and Shane's sister run to a spot near the wall and manoeuvre three benches side by side, their wooden legs screeching against the cement floor.

The four bargirls each grab a limb of Patrick and carry him to the benches, their faces scrunching with exertion. A monk steps to the four bargirls. "Here, apply some medicated oil on him. The pungent smell will wake him up."

Shane's sister takes the bottle and rubs the medicated oil on her father' temples and under his nostrils. A minute later, Patrick regains consciousness. Another minute passes before he is able to get on his feet and the chanting ceremony continues.

The present...

I toss my gaze from Bali Hai Pier to Wanicha. "Why was Shane cremated here?"

"Shane's parents wanted to fulfil his wish which was not fulfilled when he was alive – to live in Thailand. Patrick signed a document for the release of Shane's body to me so that I could arrange a cremation. The embassy liaised with the hospital and everything went smoothly." She takes a sip of her latte caramel. "Shane's family flew in as quickly as they could. After the cremation, Shane's ashes were scattered in the sea." She wipes her upper lip with her tongue and looks at Pattaya Bay for a moment before focusing her attention back to me.

Wanicha and I are in Anytime Café and our food arrives: chocolate waffle for me and banana waffle for her. Each plate has four triangular pieces of waffle. The café is located at the end of Walking Street, near Bali Hai Pier, and throngs of tourists are taking boats to the offshore islands.

I spear a waffle and pop it into my mouth. "Are you married to that American in California?"

"No, if I were, I wouldn't return to that ago-go bar anymore." She dribbles some honey on her waffles. "In fact, this American doesn't even exist."

I wash down my waffle dollops with a swallow of coffee. "Why did Patrick blame himself for his son's suicide?"

She starts to eat her waffle, talking with her mouth full. "Shortly after the *sinsod* thing, Shane left for home, and I got a text message from Patrick. In the sms, he stated that he wanted to talk to me via webcam. A day and time was agreed."

"Oh? What transpired?"

Wanicha starts to relate her conversation with Patrick...

Wanicha starts the webcam in her laptop and, moments later, an image of a middle-aged *farang* appears on the screen in front of her. He is garbed in a sweater over a checked shirt, and the background indicates he's in his study.

"Hi there, I'm Wanicha." Her lips curve in a smile.

"Hello, my name's Patrick, and I am Shane's father." His voice is gravelly, like that of a heavy smoker's.

"How did you get my phone number?"

"I checked Shane's mobile phone bill."

"What's the purpose of this webcam meeting?"

"I understand Shane's planning to marry you. He told me he's met your parents and agreed on the *sinsod*." He folds his arms and sears her with a look. "But unfortunately, I don't approve of you becoming our daughter-in-law."

Wanicha gapes, her eyes circled in shock. "Why?"

"Shane's our only son. We're staunch Catholics and we want Shane to marry a Catholic girl and remain living with us." He hikes his chin. "Furthermore, Shane is not rich and I doubt he can make you happy. Therefore, I want you to leave him." He unfolds his arms and leans forward. "In return, I will pay you three times the amount of *sinsod* that my son has agreed to your parents. Just tell Shane you do not wish to go ahead with the wedding because another man has proposed to you."

The air thins in Wanicha's throat. "No, I love Shane. I'm not marrying him for money."

"Wanicha, Shane's mother has a heart condition and sorrow will kill her very quickly. Her heart will be crushed should Shane leave us for Thailand. Please give some sympathy for the old lady." His lips gum into a straight line for a moment. "Furthermore, if you go ahead with the wedding, I'll cut Shane out of my will and he won't get any inheritance." He forms the circle "O" with his thumb and forefinger. "Zero! Nothing! Shane won't be earning much as an English teacher in Pattaya and without any inheritance, his future won't be that bright, you understand? Wanicha, if you truly love Shane and care for his future well-being, please leave him."

A tightness in Wanicha's chest surfaces, which nearly chokes her. "That's blackmail."

"You can call it whatever you want. Once you've made a decision, text me your bank account details and I'll wire the money to you. It'll be three times the amount of *sinsod* promised to your parents. That's all I want to say. Now, I'd like a favour from you, please. Don't ever tell Shane we spoke on the webcam. I don't want him to hate me. So decide wisely." He pauses. "Goodbye."

* * *

The astonishing number of foreigners committing suicide in Pattaya is a phenomenon as strange as the disappearances of aircraft over the Bermuda Triangle. The most common method among the victims is leaping off the balcony of a tall building. The high number of deaths over the past decade has earned Pattaya the moniker "Suicide Capital of Southeast Asia." However, there has been speculation that some of the deaths were murders or accidents. Below are some of the more recent cases compiled from various sources, and there are many others that have not been reported.

November 2018

On November 14, police was called to retrieve a shirtless body spotted hanging by a rope over the rooftop of a condominium block in Soi 5, off Beach Road. One end of the rope was tied to the deceased's neck and the other end to a fire hydrant on the rooftop. The victim was later identified as Max Holden, a 69-year-old Norwegian, who was married to a Thai woman. Police found a suicide note written in Norwegian, a home-made shotgun and a blood-stained chopping block on the rooftop. There was no sign of any struggle and police suspected that the victim shot himself with the shotgun before throwing himself over the rooftop.

September 2018

September 3: a security guard found the dead body of 80-year-old French citizen, Michel Hostaillier, lying on the ground at his condominium block in Jomtien Beach. He was believed to have jumped from his 17th floor balcony. His live-in boyfriend, 38-year-old Siwaporn Pala, who arrived at the scene cried hysterically and fainted and had to be revived by paramedics. Later, Siwaporn told police that he and Michel had been living together for more than a year. On that particular morning when he left the condo to pray at a temple, Michel appeared normal though he was having problems with his ex-wife in France. According to police, a suicide note written in French was left by the deceased, and there were no signs of any violence in the condo.

May 2018

A hefty divorce settlement and expensive monthly alimony to his ex-wife – a former Pattaya bargirl – drove 68-year-old John Edward Charles to leap to his death from his 18th floor unit in Lumpini Ville Naklua Condominium. According to Narita Daosi, the deceased's 49-year-old wife, John arrived in Pattaya in 2011. In 2012, he met his former wife and they got married a month later. During their marriage, he kept showering her with expensive gifts. Six years later, when they divorced, he had exhausted all his life savings. Narita, who owns a coffee shop, ended up supporting John financially. A few days before his suicide, she noticed that he was always going to the balcony and looking down.

March 2018

Danish tourist Michael Peter Terkildsen, aged 52, was found dead in a parking lot after having jumped from the 34th floor of his 44-story condominium in Pattaya Road 2. He had been living there with his Thai wife for three years. According to farang-deaths.com/case/michael-peter-terkildsen: "'But that was only half of the story,' Pol. Lt. Narong warned. 'According to the testimony of several of Mr. Terkildsen's friends, she had deceived him for financial reasons.' In the end, Mr. Terkildsen lost over 3 million baht – money that was meant to cover his expenses in his adopted country." Pattayapeople.com (March 2, 2018 posting) added that police found a suicide note that said: "I do not wish to live anymore because I am broke and penniless."

February, 2018

Upon investigating a report of a foul smell coming from a condominium unit in Soi Arunatai, police discovered the naked body of Frenchman Alain Georges Robert Recon, aged 54, in his bed. It was estimated that he had been dead for at least five days as his stomach was bloated. Body-building drugs were found in the room but there were no signs of any struggle to suggest foul play. A spokesman for the condominium management told police that the deceased, a freelance dance instructor, had been living alone since renting the unit three months ago and was often seen exercising in the swimming pool area.

January, 2018

When police found the body of Frank Glas Fischer, a 40-year-old German tourist, they were investigating two possibilities: either suicide or murder. The deceased was found lying on a lonely walking trial in Khao Phra, a hilly public park, with a belt tightly tied around his neck and burn marks on his legs. The deceased's travel bag was found at a concrete stairs about 200 metres from the body. Inside the bag were some clothes, a wallet, some medications, two empty beer cans and two empty bottles of methanol. Chiangraitimes.com (Jan 5, 2018 posting) reported that: "Pol. Maj. Gen Chettha said footage from surveillance cameras in and around the area would be examined. Any people close to him they could track down would also be questioned."

August, 2017
At 2:30 a.m. on August 2, 2017, Lek Prasasit, a security guard of a condominium in Jomtien Beach, heard a loud thud like something had fallen to the ground. Upon investigating, he found a dead body. The deceased was later identified at Jamin Lee, a 23-year-old Korean, who rented an apartment on the 15th floor. According to police, CCTV footage showed that Lee left his room and walked up to the 22nd floor and from there he had apparently jumped. The victim first landed on a Honda Jazz before falling on the concrete floor in a pool of blood. Both his legs were broken and his skill fractured.

July, 2017
When a female neighbour of Hsu Tse-Hsien, a 47-year-old Taiwanese tourist, noticed a foul smell from his single-storey house and did not see him come out for several days, she called the police. Officers who arrived at the house in Chok Chai Garden Home, a gated community, forced open the front door which was

locked from the inside. A police spokesman told reporters, "When we entered the house, hundreds of flies were buzzing around our heads and the building was filled with the scent of rotting flesh. It was horrible." In the bedroom, Hsu was found dead lying face-up in bed, with the door and window closed. A pan and a stove containing charcoal ashes were found next to the bed. There was also a suicide note.

June, 2017

A South Korean man, Sang Jong Lee, aged 40, fell to his death from the 37th floor of his condominium in Soi Na Kluea 16. Pol. Lt. Patananam told reporters that the deceased had moved into the condominium only eight days earlier. He had been sent by his employer in South Korea to start work in Pattaya and was waiting for his wife to arrive. On the night of the incident, security guards noticed that the deceased appeared to be very drunk, and the next time they saw him was after he had plunged down from his balcony. For the time being, police have classified his death as an accident, unless there is new evidence to suggest otherwise.

June 2017

When Sunton, the owner of a car rental company, was alerted by his staff that a Frenchman, Michel Bachelleric, was late in returning a Toyota Corolla, he tracked down the car's location using its in-built GPS locator. When Sunton arrived at the house in Lake Valley, he found the rented car parked in the front porch and the front door of the house unlocked. When he entered the living room after calling several times, he saw a pool of blood on the floor and alerted a security guard who informed the police. According to farang-deaths.com/case/michel-bachelleric, Pol.

Capt. Kongdet Sowapat told reporters that the body of 68-year-old Michel, a retiree, was found upstairs naked on the floor next to his bed. The police officer added, "We hope the result of the autopsy will help us find out what happened to him."

May 2017

When the Thai wife of Raymond Charles Britland, aged 69, came home from work, she was shocked to find her husband dead in their bathroom. There was a lot of blood on the floor and walls. Mrs. Somapon Britland, aged 46, and her husband lived in a gated community in Nong Prue, and had been married for 18 years. Mrs. Somapon told police that her husband had been depressed because of ill health and high medical bills. According to the police, Raymond had a deep cut in his left wrist and a razor was found beside his body. An investigation of the bathroom and other rooms in the house did not indicate any foul play.

April 2017

Tourists strolling along Walking Street at 4:30 a.m. were horrified when a naked male body fell from the third-storey balcony of Darling Guest House (not its real name) to the pavement. The victim, later identified as Andrew Christopher Laidler, a 31-year-old Briton, was given first aid and rushed to Pattaya Memorial Hospital, but he died shortly after admission. Police officers who inspected his room said there was no sign of a struggle and his belongings were intact. They added they would question staff of the guest house and examine CCTV footage in the area.

June 2016

A year earlier, Darling Guest House at Walking Street was the scene of another death when a *farang* was found naked and dead in his room. He had no identification papers with him and his wallet was missing, so he was sent to a police morgue in Bangkok. A ladyboy who was with him before his death was questioned by the police. Later, the deceased was identified as Steve Balfour, a 35-year-old Scottish ex-soldier, by a distinctive tattoo on his arm. A month ago, Steve was reported missing when he took leave from his job as a security consultant to fly to Pattaya to visit his ex-Thai wife and six-year-old daughter Christina and did not return as scheduled. He and his ex-wife had divorced the previous year.

* * *

Somchair, the twenty-something bartender, squirts a spray of yellowish liquid from a bottle of sanitizer onto the top of a bar table. With a white cloth, he wipes the liquid all over the table. He moves to the next table and repeats the process. As he works from the front of the hall to the back, he sees Noah, the owner, sitting at a writing desk in one corner and doing the business accounts.

Wearing a hangdog expression, Noah is checking stacks of suppliers' invoices and order chits and tapping keys on his laptop, which is running his accounting software. Aged forty, he has a square jaw, a broad nose and wavy brown hair.

Somchair moves to the bar and starts to sanitize it. As he moves the white cloth in circular motions, he peers at his employer from the corner of his eye. *Oh dear, business has not been good and the bar's losing money. I hope I don't lose my job.* He sees his boss scrub his worrisome face with his hand. Then, Noah pushes himself from the desk to sink back in the low-backed swivel chair and pinches his eyes shut as if to hatch a plan to bring in more business. Somchair sucks in a deep inhale and exhales in despair. *Poor man, failure is etched on every line on his face. He has lost whatever spark he once had when he first came to Pattaya five years ago.*

Half an hour later, Somchair catches a glimpse of a woman outside the front glass door jabbing buttons on the access control panel. Moments later, the plastic CLOSED sign clatters against the glass door as it swings inward. In steps a Thai woman of about thirty years old. *Oh, my boss's wife is here.* She is dressed in a long turquoise sheath dress that accentuates her slender body. In the crook of her left hand dangles the straps of a small shopping bag. She wends her way on sandals between bar tables and goes to sit at a chair across Noah's desk.

"Good afternoon, Urassaya." The edges of Somchair's mouth crooks in a smile.

Urassaya casts a sideway glance at the bartender. "Afternoon, Somchair." She focuses her attention back to Noah. "How's the new accounting software? User-friendly?" She has heavy eyebrows and her thick lips complement her oval face.

Noah looks away from the laptop screen. "What brings you here?"

"I went to the temple and got a statue of Nang Kwak, the Thai Goddess of Wealth." She dips her hand in the shopping bag and takes out a five-inch porcelain statue depicting a Thai lady in traditional costume. "You should fix a ledge shelf on the wall that faces the front entrance and place the statue on it." She hands the statue over to Noah. "Pray to the goddess every morning and business should improve. I'll go buy joss sticks and a small copper urn later."

Holding the statue in one hand, Noah casts a curious gaze at it. "Why is her right hand in a waving position? It reminds me of maneki-neko, the Japanese Beckoning Cat."

"Exactly! Her right hand beckons wealth and customers to a business. In fact, she has been nicknamed the Beckoning Lady."

"I see." He puts the statue on top of a glass paper weight at one corner of the desk. "Let me put this aside for the time being. I'll install the ledge shelf in a couple of days' time." He yanks open the top right hand drawer, takes out several small sheets of paper held together by a paper clip and slips them in front of Urassaya. "Since you're here, I want you to run a few errands for me." He wrenches out his wallet from his trouser's side pocket. "Please pay the water bill, electricity bill and fire insurance premium." He takes out some money notes and counts them. "Here's the cash." He hands over the money.

"Okay, I'll do it right away."

A week later...

Garbed in jeans and a t-shirt, Noah is sitting on the marble floor of a prayer hall facing a statue of Lord Buddha in a small lesser-known temple. His eyes are closed and he appears to be meditating. Outside, the sweltering sun is making heat waves rise from the concrete compound.

A minute later, a Thai man enters the prayer hall and kneels at an arm's length away from Noah. The Thai man harrumphs.

Noah opens his eyes and peers at the man from the corner of one eye. "Are you Preecha?" The man is sporting penitentiary hair cut and tattoos are peeking out from under his rolled-up sleeves

"You're Noah?" His guttural voice is a half-whisper.

"That's right."

Preecha turns his head sideways to look at Noah. "Our friend says you have a job for me?"

Noah looks straight ahead at the statue of Lord Buddha. "I want you to set fire to a bar." He casts a quick side glance at Preecha. "Can you handle the job?"

"It's your bar, right?"

"Yes."

Preecha's lips curve into a knowing smile. "I see – for the insurance money." The smile disappears. "Of course, I can do it."

A price is agreed which will be paid upon completion of the job.

Lying on his left side on his bed, Noah stares in anticipation at the alarm clock on his bedside table. *If Preecha has succeeded, there should be a call from someone soon.* Light from a lamp is casting a yellow circle on the bedside table. Also lying within the yellow circle is his mobile phone which is switched on. Beside him on the bed, Urassaya is sleeping soundly, curled up in a fetal position, her silk nightgown clinging loosely to her curvy body.

An hour passes. Noah is almost dozing off when his mobile rings. Blinking away the sleepiness, he picks it up and answers the call. "Hello?" He manoeuvres to a sitting position. "Yes, I am Noah...Huh? My God! When did it happen? Has the fire been put out? Hmmm...I see. Thank you, thank you so much."

Urassaya stirs in her sleep, blinking and rubbing her eyes. "*Thirak* [darling], what's going on?"

"Our bar burned down!" *Hooray!* "Totally destroyed!"

Urassaya pushes herself to a sitting position. "Oh, my goodness!" Her eyes span wider in shock. "Oh, hell, now I remember! Oh no!"

"No big deal, darling." He clamps his lips to stifle a smirk. "The bar's covered by fire insurance."

"No, it's not!" Her face is sculpted in panic. "Oh Lord Buddha! What've I done?"

"What do you mean by that? Two weeks ago, I asked you to pay the fire insurance premium didn't I?"

Urassaya's chin starts to quiver. "On that day, after I paid the electricity and water bills, I went to browse in Siam Paragon. A few handbags and clothes caught my fancy. I used the cash for the fire insurance premium to buy those items. I - I planned to use my own money to pay the premium later, but I procrastinated and forget about it!" Her moist eyes seem to plead for forgiveness. "Oh, I'm so sorry, I really am."

The air suspends in Noah's throat and blood drains from his face, making him feel dizzy.

The present...

Somchair takes a drag of his cigarette. "The next day after the fire, Noah committed suicide by jumping from his condo's balcony." Streams of smoke float upward from Somchair's nostrils, resembling elephant tusks.

I pick up a groundnut and crack it open. "When did this incident happen?" I pop the seeds into my mouth and chew them.

"About five, six years ago."

I suck a sip of my Coca-Cola through the straw in my glass. "How did you know that Preecha was hired by Noah?" I thud my elbows on the table and clasp my hands together.

Somchair rests his cigarette on the edge of a Remy Martin ash tray. "That gangster Preecha came to Noah's wake. He pulled

Urassaya to a corner, told her his arrangement with Noah and demanded payment." He picks up a groundnut and cracks it. "I overheard everything Preecha said. Urassaya didn't believe him and refused to pay. After an argument, Preecha left the wake." He finds that the groundnut is empty and tosses the shells away.

"What happened to the destroyed bar?"

"I don't know. A week after the fire, I was lucky to get a new job in another part of town." He picks up his cigarette from the ash tray, slips it between his lips and draws in a lungful of smoke. "Months later, when I passed my former work-place, I saw that a new bar had come up."

4

Sea, Sand and Sex

The waves in the ocean are crested with silvery foam as the rays of the sun glistens on them. I am strolling down a shady palm-lined stretch on Jomtien Beach with the breezes caressing my face and the roar of water scooters assaulting my ear-drums. Scattered on the rust-coloured sands are pot-bellied men and pear-shaped women lying on towels to sunbathe. Under colourful umbrellas, foot-massage women are waiting for customers under the shade of palm trees, their leaves swaying in the wind.

As I'm passing her spot, a woman sitting on a stool stationed at the end of the footrest of a deck chair asks "Pedicure and foot massage, sir?" Her pronunciation is near-faultless and she is garbed in a sarung, a broad-rim hat and a pair of shades.

I stop in my tracks. "How much?"

She removes her shades and places them on her sarung-covered lap. "Five hundred baht for pedicure and massage and fifty baht for rental of chair."

From her chocolate-complexioned face shine a pair of lively eyes, and I guess that she's in her thirties.

"Where're you from?"

"Chanthaburi Province."

Aha! That's interesting. What brought her here? "I'll pay you six hundred baht if you tell me your life story. I like to listen to interesting stories – deal?"

"Yup, it's a deal!" The corners of her lips upturn in a smile. "Come, sit down" She gestures with an open palm to the deck chair and fishes out a pair of surgical gloves from a basket at her side. "What do you want me to talk about?" She slips on her surgical gloves and takes out a pair of nail clippers.

I kick off my slippers and move to recline on the deck chair. "What's your name? And what made you come here to work in foot massage?"

"Antika." She starts to clip my toe nails.

A village in Chanthaburi Province, fifteen years ago...

Thirty-something-year-old Basor steers his motorbike over chilli-brown-coloured grounds to an area of the durian plantation where trees grow to great heights. Sitting behind him is his young assistant with an oblong-shaped rattan basket strapped to his back. Two days ago, Basor, a vegetable farmer, secured a contract to harvest fruits for the owner of the durian plantation.

Presently, Basor stops his motorbike below a tree and he and his passenger alight. He scans the branches of the tree and sees several ripe fruits. Kicking off his slippers, he shimmies up its trunk and climbs up to a branch where several durians are hanging from stalks on a higher branch. Meanwhile, his assistant is standing below, holding the oblong-shaped rattan basket by its handles. As Basor cuts the stalk of a fruit with a penknife, it drops to the waiting basket held by his assistant. One by one, the fruits are harvested in this manner and they are gathered at a shady spot nearby.

Basor walks to the next nearest tree and looks up where morning sunlight is bursting through gaps in the leaves, twigs and branches. He lifts one hand to shade his eyes from the glare as he searches for ripe fruits. *Thump!* "Ugh!" grunts Basor, collapsing to the ground and passing out, his head bleeding.

"My goodness, a falling durian landed on his head!" His assistant's eyes widen in horror. "Hell, it's bigger than a soccer ball!" He rushes to Basor's motorcycle and rides off to get help.

Eight days later...

Morning brings another day to the Basor household comprising thirteen-year-old Antika, two sons and his wife. The crowing of the rooster from the chicken coop sounds like the creaking of a rusty door hinge ending with someone's groan. Inside her bedroom in the farm house which has a window facing the chicken coop, Antika gets out of her bed and goes to the bathroom to brush her teeth. In the adjacent room, Antika's older brother and younger brother, fifteen and ten years old respectively, yawn and stretch as they shake off their sleepiness. In a short while, after their breakfast, they will walk to their respective schools. Antika, on the other hand, has never been to school.

Exiting the farm house through the back door, Antika goes to the chicken coop, which comprises a high wire-netting fence enclosing a rectangular area the size of a badminton court with a wooden shed standing in the centre. She pushes the Z-frame wire-netting gate at the fence open, treads gingerly past speckles of chicken faeces on the ground to the door of the shed and opens it. Dozens of chickens scurry out, apparently happy to be released. Antika enters the shed and takes a bucket hanging at the back of the door. From a barrel in a corner, she scoops up chicken feed and fills up a third of the bucket. As always, the foul smell of the feed makes her wince. She goes outside to the open area and scatters the feed on the ground. As squawking chickens scratch and peck at the feed on the ground, Antika re-enters the shed, collects eggs from nests and puts them in a rattan basket. Carrying the basket, she barrels through the back door of the farm house that leads to the kitchen with her hip to go inside.

"How many eggs today?" asks *Mae,* standing at a sizzling pan on a gas-stove and stirring its contents with a wooden ladle.

Antika puts the basket on the grey cement floor in one corner of the kitchen. "Fourteen." She goes to the wooden dining table where a bowl of her vegetable *joke* [gruel] is waiting. Two empty bowls filled with the dregs of *joke* indicate that her brothers have finished their breakfast and have left for school.

Her *Mae* looks over her shoulder to her daughter. "Antika, your *Phx* wants to talk with you. Two days ago, he and I discussed something important." The tone of her voice is tight with tension. "After you've finished eating, can you go to his room?"

"Yes, *Mae.*"

Antika raps a few times on the wooden door, swings it open and enters her father's bedroom. Discharged from hospital four days ago, Basor is leaning on two pillows propped against the headboard. He looks like a turbaned Sikh with his head swathed in thick bandages.

Antika goes to sit on the edge of his bed. "*Phx,* how's your injury?" Her eyes brim with sympathy.

Basor stares at the opposite wall with a glazed look. "The wound will heal, but the concussion damaged my optic nerves. I'm now permanently blind."

"What! This is terrible!" Wetness shimmers in Antika's eyes. "Oh, *Phx,* I'm so sad." Her voice suddenly turns rusty, as if she's sick.

Basor expends a weary sigh. "*Mae* and I have decided that you should go stay with my brother-in-law in Pattaya." He extends a groping hand. "He runs a sundry store and needs additional workers." He finds Antika's hand and holds it. "*Mae* has bought a bus ticket for you and she has informed my brother-in-law of your arrival. Your trip to Pattaya is tomorrow by the 10 a.m. bus. Tonight, *Mae* will guide my hand to write my brother-in-law's address. Tomorrow, I'll give you some money as tuk-tuk fare, and my friend will come fetch you to the bus station on his motorbike." His words start to come out half-choked. "When you are in Pattaya bus station, show the address to any tuk-tuk driver and he will take you there." He pats her hand a few times. "After you complete your chores, pack some clothes for tomorrow's journey. My brother-in-law will take good care of you."

"Yes, *Phx*."

After a three-hour journey, Antika climbs down from the bus which has stopped in a parking bay outside the terminal building on North Pattaya Road. She scrunches her nose as exhaust fumes drift around her and her eyes squint to adjust to the hot afternoon sun. Carrying a small reed bag in one hand, she steps inside the terminal building – a giant roof propped up by several huge steel pillars – and finds herself surrounded by people milling around and rows and rows of plastic chairs. Almost overwhelmed by the noise, she crosses the terminal building to the other side and walks down a road where a few tuk-tuks are waiting in a line.

Antika saunters to the first tuk-tuk, rounds the front to the driver's side where a young skinny man is sitting in the cabin. "Mister," she says through the rolled-down window, "can you please take me to this address?" From her reed bag, she plucks out a piece of paper which has been folded trice and held together by a toothpick.

The driver sticks his hand out the window, takes the paper and pulls out the toothpick. "Where are you from?"

"A village in Chanthaburi Province."

The driver reads what's written on the paper and his brows bunch up. "Sorry, I cannot take you there." He re-folds the paper, pierces the toothpick back in the holes and returns it to Antika.

"Why? I've money to pay you."

"I can't take you there." The driver gives a gentle shake of his head. "Don't ask me why."

Inside the cabin of his tuk-tuk, Mr. Beefy is sitting with his right leg resting on his left knee when a teenage girl dressed in a frumpy dress saunters towards him. Earlier, he saw the girl approach the tuk-tuk parked in front of him. *I wonder why the first driver doesn't want to fetch her?* He tilts his head sideways. "Yes? Where do you want to go?"

"I want to go to my relative's house." The girl dips into her bag, takes out a few coins and shows them to Mr. Beefy. "I've money for your fare." She replaces the coins and takes out a folded piece of paper. "This is his address." She thrusts her hand through the rolled-down window.

Mr. Beefy takes the paper, plucks out the toothpick and reads the Thai scripts scribbled on it:

Please send this girl to the nearest orphanage.

We've no money to raise her.

Your kindness will earn you good merits.

Thank you so much.

Mr. Beefy's heart almost stalls in his chest. *Oh, Lord Buddha!*

She has such heartless parents! "Alright, I will take you there."
A heave of pity causes his breath to choke in his throat. "Please
keep your money – there's no need to pay me any fare." *I'll let the
orphanage people explain her situation to her – I don't have the
heart to do it.* "Come inside and sit in the passenger seat."

Sitting on a rattan chair in the living room, Basor hears the
grandfather clock hanging on the wall chime one o'clock. *Antika
has reached Pattaya already. I hope an orphanage will accept her.*
As his wife has left to work on the vegetable plots and his sons
have yet to return from school, the house is enveloped in silence.
He puts a hand to his face, his chest heaving, and a twinge of guilt
tightens his heart.

Minutes pass. Like a trapped rat trying to escape, his mind
seeks solace by recalling his wizened friend's advice when the
latter visited him in hospital several days ago. "Basor," said his
friend with a white beard resembling the archetypal wise old man,
"it is your two sons who will take care of you in future. If you
want to let go of one of your children, it should be your daughter.
When a daughter marries, her priority is to her husband and
family, not her parents anymore. A son's responsibility is to care
of his parents even after his marriage."

The words repeat themselves like a needle stuck in the groove
of a gramophone record until they assuage his guilt and, finally,
he dozes off.

Seven years later...
Growling synthesizer bass and funky drum beats boom inside the
ago-go bar. Lights flash, sparkle and twinkle. A hoarse voice yells,
"Put your fucking hands up!" A flurry of hands from eight ago-

go dancers wave in the air. Dressed in bikinis with numbers on badges as identification, they gyrate atop a central stage in the hall. On two sides of the hall are banquettes which are occupied by more than twenty men of different nationalities.

The mamasan ambles on wedges past the men on one banquette. "Sir, pick your lady! Pick your lady!"

Unable to close any sale, she proceeds to the banquette on the opposite side, moving past the men one by one and jabbering "Come on, choose your lady! They're all very friendly!"

Ted, a mid-thirties divorcee from Melbourne, runs his gaze over the bodies of the eight ago-go dancers, his crotch throbbing. *The girl wearing glow-in-the dark condoms around her wrists knows her stuff! She stands out among the rest in terms of looks.* When the mamasan approaches him, he hikes his chin and hollers, "Number six – long-time barfine!"

"That's Antika! An excellent choice, sir!" The mamasan's lips zag into a smile. "She gives high GFE. Long-time bar fine is five thousand baht!" She extends her palm. "Money, please!"

Another year later...
Ted casts his gaze from the crescent bay of Pattaya to Antika's eyes. "Antika, I'd like to meet your parents." He takes a sip of his iced Cappuccino as sea breezes whisper like his lover, planting kisses on his cheeks.

"Why?" Antika pushes wisps of bangs from her eyes.

Ted and Antika are sitting at a square table at the famous viewpoint of Pratumnak Hill. Ever since they got to know each other, during Ted's return to Australia, they have been keeping in contact by email, Skype and webcam.

A smile blooms on Ted's lips. "To discuss the *sinsod*."

"What! You want to marry me?"

"Of course!" Ted takes Antika's hand, lifts it to his mouth and presses his lips to it.

"Oh *thirak*!" Hot blood whooshes to Antika's cheeks. "I'm so happy! B-but, darling, I don't feel like meeting my parents."

"I know you resent your parents but why not make peace with them since you'll be getting married?" Ted's eyes brim with gentleness. "Financial hardships forced them to make a difficult and painful decision. Forgiving them will allow you to find inner peace, and move ahead with your life." The tone of his voice lowers to a solemn level. "Didn't Buddha say that 'to understand everything is to forgive everything.' "

"Oh, Ted, you're getting philosophical again." Antika locks gazes with Ted. "Yes, on second thought, it'll be good to have their blessings for our marriage." *I haven't sent any money to them since working in the bar, so Ted's sinsod will be a small windfall for them.*

"I'll rent a car and drive there. Let's go to your village during the Chanthaburi Durian Festival –we'll put up one night in a hotel."

Chanthaburi Town

Ted manoeuvres the rented Toyota Yaris into a parking bay outside King Taksin The Great Park in downtown Chanthaburi Town. As he yanks the handbrake up, Antika, sitting beside him, takes her handbag from the floor and gets out of the car.

Earlier, she directed him to her home village eight kilometres north. She found her parents' farm house but it had been sold, and another family was living there. They were unable to assist on the whereabouts of Antika's family.

Greeted by faint music, Ted and Antika stroll with linked hands under an archway with the words "Chanthaburi World Durian Festival". Jostling among the crowds, they start to explore the stalls set up on the sidewalk bordering the man-made lake. They pass stalls selling local products and souvenirs which do not interest them and proceed to the fruits section. At a stall, they stop to sample durian chips laid on a plastic platter on a makeshift sales counter. A young girl is manning the counter which is piled with plastic packets of both uncooked and fried durian chips. Nearby, an elderly woman is frying the snack in a bowl-shaped frying pan.

The crunch of the durian chips echoes in Antika's ears. "Wow! They're good!"

Ted nods, chomping with firm clamps of his jaw. "I want a few packets." He dips into his pocket for his wallet and asks the salesgirl, "How much for one packet?"

The woman behind the bowl-shaped frying pan looks up from the bubbling oil and her mouth gapes. "Oh Lord Buddha!" Her eyes circle in shock. "It's you, Antika!" She turns down the flame on the gas stove and takes several steps forward. "When did you come back?" Her tone is hesitant as she opens her outstretched arms.

Antika moves forward to swallow her in a momentary hug. "*Mae!*" The breath from her throat parts from her lips in a short shallow gasp as she pulls away and takes a step backward. "Why did you and *Phx* abandon me?" A kaleidoscope of emotions shifts across her expression, from a tinge of hurt, to relief, and finally respect.

"I'm so sorry, Antika!" Her *Mae*'s voice sounds like it's bleeding from pain. "We could not afford to raise you!" Tears skitter down her wrinkled cheeks. "Please forgive us! I know what we did was wrong."

Her words light upon Antika like a cool mist in the hot afternoon, comforting her. "Where's *Phx*?"

"Where else? Sitting at home – what can a blind man do?"

"What about Bancha and Chusak?"

"After you left for Pattaya, Bancha stopped schooling to work on the farm. He was unhappy and, two years later, he ran away. Chusak was too young for manual work so *Phx* sold the farm and we moved to a two-room flat in Chanthaburi. Then I was running a mobile food stall with Chusak as my helper. Later, he got involved with bad company and he, too, ran away. Now, I'm working for the owner of a durian plantation and *Phx* is weaving rattan baskets at home. This stall belongs to my employer." She tosses her gaze at Ted. "Who's this man?"

"*Mae*, this is my boyfriend, Ted." She latches a hand to his arm. "We're getting married soon. He wants to discuss the *sinsod* with you and *Phx*."

"Lord Buddha be praised! Our future son-in-law is rich!" A chortle rolls from Basor's lips. "With the big *sinsod* he's going to wire to us next week, I want to get a motorbike with a side carriage. Then you can fetch me around town."

Basor and his wife are lounging on the settee in their small living room, listening to music from a radio.

"I'm going to resign from that durian plantation." Mrs. Basor leans her head sideways on her husband's shoulder. "Last week, my friend told me about a half-shop for rent. I want to take it and sell cakes. Tomorrow, I'll go see the landlord and also drop by the motorbike store to book your motorbike." She reaches out to hold Basor's hand. "Hmmm...what else can we buy?"

Back in Pattaya, Ted and Antika enter the doctor's room and sits down across her at her desk. It has been several days since the couple returned from Chanthaburi and they went for a blood test.

The doctor pulls open a top drawer and takes two files. "I'm sorry – I've bad news for one of you." She hands them over separately to Ted and Antika. "One of you has a condition and cannot be a parent." She leans back in her chair, her expression crestfallen. "Please look at the blood test report."

Ted pulls out a piece of paper from his file and scans the items listed on it. *Full Blood Count... Differential Blood Count... Cholesterol... Tumour Marker... Liver Function Profile... Renal Function Profile...VDRL: Non reactive... HIV: Positive.* Shock almost stills the blood in his veins. "Jesus Christ! I'm damned!"

"What's the matter, darling?"

"I can't marry you, Antika!" Ted's pulse throbs in his ears. "I'm HIV positive."

"Oh Lord Buddha, that's a double blow for me!" Antika's face contorts in despair. "My parents will lose their deposits for the things they've ordered."

A month later...
Antika strides on stilettos to the bar and says to the bartender. "Paitoon, give me a glass of whisky, please." She is garbed in a bikini with a dark wraparound skirt.

The goateed bartender wearing crew-cut turns to a cabinet behind him, takes out a bottle of Sangsom Whisky and pours a splash into a shot glass filled with ice cubes. He slides the glass to Antika's waiting hand.

Without uttering a word, she slams the shot of whisky to the back of her throat. "Another shot, please."

Paitoon refills the glass, his gaze studying her. *Oh dear, ever since her marriage plan failed, she's been very depressed.*

Eyes glazed, Antika turns around to scan the patrons seated in the hall, brings the glass to her lips and takes a glug. Moments pass. Now, she turns her attention to the DJ moving his head from side to side behind his console packed with blinking lights. Then she empties her glass in a swallow, returns her attention to the bartender and plunks the glass down. "Refill, please." She pushes the glass towards him.

The bartender scratches the back of his head. "Again?"

"Yes, please." Antika's voice is deadpan.

The bartender pours another shot into her glass and slides it to her. Before Antika can reach for her glass, a hand wearing gold rings on two fingers snatches it away. She turns to see that the drink-snatcher is Mummy.

"You sure you can dance?" Mummy's eyes shine with a stern twinkle. "You're up in fifteen minutes' time."

"Don't worry, Mummy. I'll be fine."

Mummy crimps her brows, her voice laced with concern. "But what about riding your moped home?"

"I've been riding a moped for years."

"Come, snap out of your depression." Mummy returns the drink to Antika. "You'll meet someone new soon – perhaps someone even better."

Four hours later...

The bars, stores and restaurants on both sides of the road ahead blurs as the moped picks up speed. The night wind cools Antika's face, the sputtering of the moped's engine – muffled under her helmet – sounds like a distant freight train, her fingers gripping the throttle quiver, her temples throb as fast as the piston in the moped's engine.

The moped zooms out of the city and old buildings whizz by on both sides. The surface of the road becomes rougher, but Antika does not feel it: she feels like her machine is hovering inches above the road. In the rearview mirror, she spots a car coming up behind her but her alcohol-sodden senses make her ignore it.

At the next intersection, a tuk-tuk cruises across. *Dammit!* Half-lidded eyes widened in shock, Antika swerves to the right to avoid the tuk-tuk. Her sandal-shod foot jams down on the brake pedal and her rear wheel skids, causing the moped to lose balance. A honk behind her blasts in her ear drums. The moped falls. *Arrrrrgh!* She soars through the air, the tarred road flying upward to her face. Her heart batters against her rib cage. The sound of metal tearing and scraping is the last thing she hears before she passes out after hitting the road.

Back to the present...

I wince as Antika digs her thumbs into my sole. "Why did you turn to reflexology after the accident?"

Releasing my foot, Antika lifts up her sarung and tosses her gaze at her own legs. "See?" My jaw drops. Her left leg has been amputated below the knee! "Who wants to go out with one-legged bargirl? The car ran over my left leg and the doctors could not save it." She points at the sandy ground under the deck chair I'm reclining on. "My crutches are under your deck chair."

"Where're your parents now?"

"My father died of stomach cancer two years after my

accident. According to my *Mae*, he died a painful death. He could not afford pain killers as I couldn't send him much money." She wipes beads of sweat on her forehead with her sleeve. "I don't know, but maybe, his death was the result of bad karma." She continues the foot massage. "My mother told him that his dying words were 'I should have abandoned my sons instead of my daughter.'"

* * *

Thirty-year-old Cowan Cheah (not his real name), an IT consultant of Clementi, Singapore, strolls out his hotel at Beach Road with twenty-five-year-old social escort Samorn, whose 36-24-36 figure has made several men thrown lingering stares at her and knocking into lamp posts.

Walking hand-in-hand, they cross the road to a jet ski station under a grove of coconut trees.

"Want to rent jet ski?" asks a scrawny man.

"You have a double-seater?"

"Yes!" Mr. Scrawny's eyes gleam with eagerness. "We have a double-seater. Only eight thousand baht for one hour."

"Great! I'll take it."

Mr. Scrawny whips out a clipboard with a piece of paper on top. "Please write your full name, hotel name and room number." He pulls out a ballpoint pen from his back pocket.

"What's this?"

Mr. Scrawny holds the clipboard level in front of Cowan. "Just a disclaimer that we're not liable for any accidents."

Cowan scribbles on the paper. From his side trouser pocket, he pulls out his wallet wrapped in a plastic bag and unfastens the rubber band tied around it. He takes out some money, reseals the wallet with the plastic bag and hands over the payment.

"Thank you, sir!" Mr. Scrawny steps to a chair with several life jackets stacked on top. He takes two life jackets and passes them to Cowan. "Please wear them."

Sitting on the jet ski, Cowan and Samorn glide over the waves with whoops and shrieks. Their hour passes as quickly as the banana boats whizzing around. Cowan manoeuvres the jet ski to the beach. He kills the engine and clambers down.

Mr. Scrawny hurries to the jet ski and points to its left bow. "Hey! There's a crack here! You must have hit a rock!" He walks round the machine to inspect it. "Oh Lord Buddha, a small piece has broken off at this side! Mister, you must pay compensation for the damage!"

Two men with arms covered with tattoos appear from behind the coconut grove and approach Mr. Scrawny who jabbers in Thai language and points out the damage to the jet ski. "I think ten thousand baht is needed for repair," says one of the tattooed men to Mr. Scrawny.

Mr. Scrawny turns to Cowan. "My partner says compensation is ten thousand."

"Cut the crap!" Samorn pulls out her mobile phone from the back pocket of her shorts and unwraps the outer plastic paper. She taps a few buttons and images appear on the screen. "See?" She thrusts her phone in Mr. Scrawny's face. "While you were busy with my boyfriend, I took photos of your jet ski. The damage to your jet ski is already there before we rented it!" She puts her mobile phone away and berates the tree men in Thai language. Turning to Cowan, she says, "Come, darling, let's go. They're just scammers."

* * *

Sitting on an upended beer crate, massage boy Jakkri, aged twenty-six, casts his gaze from a man parasailing through the sky thirty feet above the choppy sea to a fellow masseuse to his left, lounging on a deck chair under shady palms on the beach. A squat Japanese man is talking with him, and after several seconds, he walks away and starts to saunter in the direction of Jakkri, whose sleeveless singlet is rolled up midway up his chest, revealing lean six-pack abs.

Cast by the afternoon sun, the long shadow of the Japanese man with a bulbous head soon falls on the sands at Jakkri's feet. "Massage, sir?" asks Jakkri with a smile, revealing small even teeth.

"No, thank you." The Japanese man, probably mid-thirties, smiles back, turning his small eyes into slits. "But would you like to earn some extra money?" He has on a short-sleeved floral print shirt and long slacks.

"Oh?" Eyes opening wider, Jakkri sits up straighter. "How?"

"Would you like to act in a Japanese A.V.?"

Jakkri blinks his big, round eyes. "What's A.V.?"

"Adult video." The Japanese man pushes aside a curtain of hair, tousled over his forehead by the wind.

"What!" Jakkri parts his mouth in surprise. "You recruit porn actors by approaching strangers?"

"Yes, this is one of the ways talent scouts do it in Japan." The Japanese man pulls out a wallet from his side pocket and slips out a shiny card. "Here's my business card. My name's Kenichi Furukawa (a pseudonym), Casting Director." He returns his wallet back into his side pocket. "I'm staying at the Phra

Chonburi Resort. Come see me tomorrow if you're interested. But give me a call first, okay?"

"Was that massage boy you spoke to earlier interested?"

"Nope, he said he's too shy." Kenichi's thick lips upturn in a scowl. "Silly boy!"

Jakkri strides along the carpeted corridor to the business centre of Phra Chonburi Resort, pushes the frosted glass open and enters. "Yes?" asks a young woman wearing a blazer and a knee-length skirt seated behind a small desk.

Earlier Jakkri phoned Kenichi and the latter told him to meet in the business centre of the hotel.

"I'm looking for Mr. Furukawa."

The woman gestures with an open palm to a door with the sign Meeting Room to her left. "Inside there."

Jakkri knocks once, pushes the door open and steps inside a small room. Sitting at a desk, Kenichi Furukawa flicks his gaze up from the screen of the laptop in front of him.

"Good afternoon, Mr. Kenichi Furukawa."

"Just call me Kenichi." Kenichi pushes his laptop to one side. "Sit down, please."

"What's your name?"

"Jakkri." He drags out a chair and sits opposite Kenichi. "Can you tell me more about this A.V.?"

"Sure." Kenichi leans back and rests his pudgy hands on the arms of the chair. "First, let me introduce our company. It's called Ogazumu Studio (not its real name), now six years old already. This is a legit porn company based in Tokyo. We're going to shoot an adult video here. Location will be an isolated beach on one of the small islands off Pattaya. Sex-in-the-bedroom is old hat so we're trying sex-on-the-beach to test the market."

"Err, why can't shooting be done in Japan?"

"It's autumn now back home," Kenichi gives a gentle shake of his bulbous head, "so it's too cold." He clears his throat. "Now the story line of this video is simple. Two Japanese women come to Thailand for vacation. One of them meets a beach bum. One thing leads to another and, eventually, they have sex. She is satisfied and returns with her friend for a threesome. There will be a short break between the two scenes." He lifts up a slender briefcase resting near his right foot on the floor and places it on his lap. "Running time is one hour." He opens the lid of the briefcase a crack. "So, you've to stretch the two acts to one hour – that means performing foreplay, oral sex, and whatever is necessary, understand?" He pulls out a sheet of paper and hands it to Jakkri. "Here's the script in English. You can improvise some additional lines if you want to." He pulls out another sheet of paper, places it in front of him and returns the briefcase to the floor.

Jakkri scans the paper and casts his gaze upward to Kenichi. "It's pretty straightforward."

Kenichi pulls out a ballpoint pen from his shirt pocket. "You think you can handle the role?" He places the pen beside the paper in front of him.

"Of course! But how much is the pay?"

"Three thousand Japanese yen. That's about eight hundred Thai baht."

"What! So little?" Jakkri curls his lips in a sneer. "You're crazy! No way!"

"Then how much do you want?" asks Kenichi with a thrust of his jaw.

"Six thousand Japanese yen."

"Five thousand—take it or leave it." Kenichi stabs Jakkri with a piercing glare. "This first-time role can lead to bigger things. Japanese talent scouts may seek you out later for other videos."

Jakkri's eyes shine with hope. "Agreed!"

Kenichi scribbles the numerals five thousand on a blank space on the paper in front of him and pushes it to Jakkri. "Write your full name on the dotted line and sign below."

Casting his gaze down at the paper, Jakkri squishes his brows. "I don't understand Japanese."

"Terms of employ are standard, just like any other work, payment in cash after completion of shooting. If you die of a heart attack during sex, we're not liable!" Kenichi chortles at his own joke. "I'd like to point out that you and your co-stars will be tested for HIV. I have HIV self-test kits with me in my room. I'll perform the test on you afterwards."

Jakkri leans forward, picks up the pen and signs his name. "Who will be my co-stars?" He pushes the paper back to Kenichi.

"They'll be arriving with our shooting crew this afternoon. Both are new faces in Japan's porn industry." Kenichi folds the paper in half. "You've to meet us at Bali Hai Pier tomorrow at 10 a.m. tomorrow." He lifts up his suitcase, opens it and slips the paper inside. "I've already chartered a boat." He rises to his feet. "Come, let's go to my room for your HIV test."

Sauntering along the pier with a knapsack on his back, Jakkri spots Kenichi further ahead and the latter waves his hand. Jakkri quickens his pace to join him. "Where's the crew?" Both men are clad in t-shirts, shorts and slippers.

"Already waiting in the boat." Kenichi starts to moves toward a side wing with metal railings. "You're five minutes late." He climbs down a flight of steps and hops into a bobbing speedboat.

Kenichi sits at the back and Jakkri settles down beside him. "My watch's running slow." As briny wind caresses his face, he slips off his knapsack and puts it on the empty space beside him.

Four women and two men are seated in front of Kenichi and Jakkri on two separate benches and the latter can only see the back of their heads. Two of the women are wearing their silver hair in a bun; the other two have black, shiny long hair tumbling down their shoulders in waves. Kenichi shows an "OK" sign – curled forefinger to thumb – to the boatman who starts the motor. With a roar, the boat heads out to sea, leaving behind a rooster tail of foam.

An hour later, the boat stops at a small uninhabited island with an arc of sandy beach backed by jungle. One by one, the two men, two long-haired women and two silvered-haired women – all Japanese – climb down from the boat. Seated at the back, Jakkri and Kenichi wait for the front passengers to get off before alighting. Everybody starts to wade in ankle-deep waters to the beach. The first silver-haired woman is carrying a movie camera tripod stand and a duffel over her back; the second crone has a camera bag slung over one shoulder, and her right hand is holding a folded reflector. The two long-haired women – both in their early thirties –and the two men, possibly in their forties, are lugging small PVC bags in their hands. The boatman starts the motor again and speeds away.

"He'll be back in four hours' time." Kenichi tells Jakkri.

Upon reaching dry ground, Kenichi hollers something in Japanese and walks to a spot under the shade of coconut trees. Everybody moves to the spot and leaves their belongings on the sandy ground. They pace around to survey the beach where every foot or so lies a shell, a dead coral fragment or a piece of driftwood. Behind the beach stands a forested hill, unmolested by civilization.

"Let's gather here, please!" Kenichi raises both arms and flaps his hands towards himself. "Let me do the introductions." The wind blows his hair in disarray and he swipes a hand through it.

The group assembles in an arc facing him with Jakkri standing an arm's length away at his side. "Everybody," says Kenichi, pointing a finger at Jakkri, "this is our male star Jakkri – only twenty-five years old and a first-timer in A.V." He pauses as a few people say "hello" to Jakkri, then gestures with an open palm to a scrawny man wearing a neatly trimmed pencil moustache. "Jakkri, this is Satoshi, our co-producer." Next, he tosses his gaze to a beefy man sporting a penitentiary haircut. "That's our director, Shintaro." He tilts his chin in the direction of the two silver-haired women, already in their seventies, their wrinkled faces mottled with age spots, and their skins hanging loose on their frames. "That's Akiko and Satomi – they're your co-stars."

"What!" Fire scorches Jakkri's cheeks. *Shit! I'm not fucking any old granny!* His scrotum shrivels.

Ploughing his hand through his unruly hair again, Kenichi gesticulates to the two thirtyish women. "Hikaru is the camerawoman and Meiko is the prop assistant." Releasing an exhale, he wipes sweat off his brows with the sleeve of his t-shirt. "Phew! It's pretty hot here." He removes his t-shirt to reveal a barrel chest covered with a black tattoo of a sword-wielding samurai.

Satoshi flicks his gaze to Shintaro. "We better cool down too." The two men start to slip their t-shirts over their heads, and Hikaru and Meiko proceed to set up the movie camera and reflector. Meanwhile, the two grannies take out compact kits from their bags and start to powder their faces.

Jakkri's eyes almost double in size from shock. Satoshi's back is decorated with the tattoo of a bug-eyed Japanese demon, while his chest has a design of a tiger's head baring its fangs. Shintaro is sporting colourful floral tattoos on the bulging left and right pectoral muscles of his chest. *Oh Lord Buddha! They're members of the yakuza!*

Gut cramping, Jakkri shuffles towards Kenichi who has stepped aside to keep his bundled t-shirt in his bag. "Err, Kenichi, why didn't you tell me my co-stars are old grannies?" The words almost garble in his throat. "And you are sure this video is going to sell?"

Kenichi closes the zipper of his bag, straightens up and turns to face Jakkri. "This video is for a niche market in Japan – for mature women." He meets Jakkri's gaze with unblinking eyes. "Your co-stars' names are in the contract. It's not my fault if you don't want to read it, isn't?" His tone of voice is matter-of-fact.

A few feet away, Shintaro claps his hands. "Ladies, let's look at the script again."

Jakkri shoots a pleading gaze at Kenichi. "C-can I cancel this job?" His breath almost petrifies in his throat. "I-I don't think I want to do it, err, don't think I can get an erection."

Ridges carve in Kenichi's brow. "It's too late to back out!"

Satoshi tosses his gaze at the two men, concern sharpening his features, the left side of his moustache twitching. "What's the problem now?"

Kenichi shows a thumb-down to Satoshi. "He says he can't get it up!"

"Luckily, I came prepared." Satoshi pulls out a blister pack of

Viagra from the side pocket of his khaki cargo shorts and holds it in front of himself. "Let's feed him one of this! We'll give him another pill for the second scene if necessary."

"No, please!" Jakkri's voice quivers. "Please don't force me to do it!" His voice trails into a near-wail.

In a flash, Kenichi darts to the back of Jakkri, grabs the latter's upper arms with his powerful hands and locks them. Jakkri twists to free himself but the grip is too strong. "No! I beg of you, no!" Terror seizes him, icing his skin.

Shintaro steps toward Jakkri and uses his gnarled hands to force the latter's jaw open. Eyes glinting with sinister, Satoshi tosses a blue pill to the back of Jakkri's throat and his gaze skitters to Akiko. "Akiko, give some water to your co-star!"

"Yes, sir." The old woman pulls out a plastic bottle from her duffel, moves towards Jakkri, still pinned in the arms of Kenichi, and pours a splash of water inside the former's open mouth.

"Swallow!" Shintaro clamps Jakkri's jaw shut and slaps him on the face. "Swallow the pill!" He grabs a handful of hair and yanks Jakkri's head backward.

Jakkri almost chokes on the water gurgling at the back of his throat. As he takes a glug so that he can breathe, the pill slides down the hatch of his gut. *Oh hell! I can't believe this is happening! I'm damned!*

Twenty minutes later, props assistant Meiko snaps a clapper board bearing the words "Beach Bum Sex: Scene 1" with a loud *clack!* and director Shintaro hollers, "Camera! Action!"

"It was a lucky escape for me!" says Kovit, squeezing my thighs with both hands as I lie on a deck chair. "Kenichi approached me first. When I rejected his offer, he went to talk with Jakkri."

He points to a group of massage boys playing volleyball further ahead on the beach. "See that guy in blue shorts? That's Jakkri!" He resumes the massage and his hands move closer to my crotch. "You gay, sir?" Now, he slips one hand inside my khaki shorts and his fingers start to wriggle through the leg hole of my briefs!

Eeeeek! Heat braising my cheeks, I leap up from my deck chair, fish out my wallet and count out some notes. I leave the payment on the deck chair and saunter away.

5

Spring Kisses, Autumn Tears

Rayong, 60 km south of Pattaya

"Now, ladies and gentlemen, proud parents and students," announces a male teacher standing at a mike on a small stage in the school hall, "our next speech-maker is Chaiporn Suparat (not his real name) of Matthayon 1." As the teacher steps aside and disappears into the left wing, applause erupts from the audience.

Hair plastered down neatly, Chaiporn, twelve years old, rises from his seat beside his mother Janjai and climbs up to the stage. Togged up in a spotless white shirt and dark-blue shorts, he moves to the standing mike and lowers it to the level of his mouth.

He takes a calming inhale and releases it. "Ladies and gentlemen and fellow students, I want to talk about the person I admire most. The person I admire most is not Aung San Suu Kyi or Nelson Mandela or The Dalai Lama though they're all winners of the Nobel Peace Prize. The person I admire most is my father Panit Suparat (not his real name)! During the day, he runs a popular *pad Thai* food cart in Pattaya. In the evening, he works as a cashier in a twenty-four hour convenience store. That means he works an incredible sixteen hours a day! It takes super-human effort to work such long hours. With his two sources of income, he provides food, clothes and shelter for me and my two younger sisters. He is unable to be here today because he's working in Pattaya now. Once a month, he comes home and brings me presents..."

Sitting in the front row, Janjai locks her gaze on Chaiporn, the innocence on his face tugging at her heart. She sees a mental image of her husband Panit and a whimpering sob breaks from her lips. Hot tears pool beneath her eyelids and she tugs out a cotton handkerchief from the back pocket of her blue jeans to blot them away.

Two years ago...

His helmet reflecting the rays of the morning sun, Panit, early thirties, eases the throttle of his motorcycle as he approaches his working place – a small fish sauce factory where he has been hired as a production worker for the past five years.

From afar, he sees that the gate is closed and three female workers are jabbering with the security guard. He stops his motorbike outside the security hut, kills the engine and gets off.

As he approaches the group of people, one of the women steps towards him. "Oh, Mr. Panit, this is terrible. The factory has closed! We've lost our jobs!"

"What!" Eyes circled in shock, Panit strides past her and moves to join the group. "What's this I hear that the factory has closed?"

The security guard tosses his gaze at Panit and pulls out an envelope from a stack in his left hand. "Mr. Panit, this is your salary cheque. You can go home. The factory has gone bankrupt." His gaze darts back to the other women. "Ladies, please leave, go home. There's nothing you can do." A noisy exhale of frustration rolls from his lips. "I'm out of a job myself! After I've given the salary cheques to everyone, I've to lock up the security hut and go look for another job."

Panit tears the envelope open, pulls out a cheque and looks at the figure on it. "What!" His chin drops. "Only one month's salary! No notice and no severance benefits?" Ire burns his cheeks to match the fire in his eyes. "Where's our boss?"

"I don't know, but I know he won't show his face here anymore. You're lucky to get one month's salary. I heard that the office peon and the delivery-van driver got only half month's pay."

"Panit, there's someone at the door!" hollers Janjai from the kitchen in their small flat.

Slumped on the cracked-vinyl couch in the living room, Panit stirs from his afternoon nap and blinks a few times before opening his eyes. He gets up from the couch, lumbers to the wooden door and opens it. Hot air whooshes in and feathers his face, making him pucker his brows.

Standing outside is his landlord, a plump middle-aged man. "Panit, your rent for last month is overdue. The current month's rent is going to be due soon." A frown darkens his cherubic face. "I phoned you several times over the past week but either you missed my calls or you deliberately ignored them." He extends a gnarled hand holding his handphone through a gap in the grille door. "See the call list on the screen?" He shoves his handphone in Panit's face. "Come on, at least have the courtesy to answer my calls, will you?"

"I – I'll pay you later – two months' rent at one go." His wavering voice brims with worry.

The landlord retracts his arm and slips his handphone into the side pocket of his trousers. "I heard your employer's fish sauce factory has shut down. So, how will you pay two months' rent?

Sell *pad Thai* like your late mother used to do?" A sinister glint shines from his eyes. "I'll evict you forcibly if I don't get payment by the end of the month, you hear?"

That same evening, during dinner, Janjai asks her husband, "Any luck with the interviews you've attended so far?" She waits for an answer but when there is none, she continues, "This morning, Chaiporn asked for some money to buy new exercise books. Boonsri also asked for her school bus fare."

Panit feels a boulder in his gut. "Maybe our landlord is right. Perhaps I should sell *pad Thai* as a temporary measure until I land a job." He releases a huff of frustration. "Tomorrow, I'll go rent a mobile food cart. Afterwards, I'll search for my mother's recipe. Her *pad Thai* was famous in Rayong."

Two weeks later...

A spoonful of green curry-drenched rice arrives in Janjai's mouth and she starts to chew. "How's the *pad Thai* business?" She casts her gaze at her husband seated across her at the dining table.

"Not so good." Panit stares at the dishes in front of him, his appetite elsewhere. "This is a small town."

Janjai takes a hard swallow. "I was thinking, maybe I should go to Pattaya to work."

Panit spears a fried squid ring. "What about the kids?" He pops it into his mouth

"Send Chaiporn to my parents, send one girl to my brother and the other girl to someone on your family's side. We can tell them the arrangement is only temporary. Once you get a proper job, we'll take them back."

"And what work will you do in Pattaya?"

"I heard that a bargirl in Pattaya can earn quite a lot."

"What!" sputters Panit, shards of shock slicing his stomach. "No! No! No way!" Morsels of squid meat drop from his mouth, landing on his plate below.

Dropping her fork and spoon, Janjai lashes her chin up. "Then, what's the solution to our money problem?" Her voice is edged with annoyance.

Panit's eyes wander into a faraway stare for a few moments. "I know the solution." His pulse becomes sporadic as realization throbs in his mind. "I'll go to Pattaya to work instead. I'll sell *pad Thai* during the day and take a second job in the evening." His tone of voice is nonchalant but a muscle in his neck twitters. "I'll pack some clothes afterwards, including the cooking utensils. Tomorrow, I'll leave by the earliest possible bus." A raspy sigh wrenches from his lips.

Pattaya

Sitting in his office room, Kiattisak, the beer-bellied owner of Hard Horny Bar (not its real name), is perusing his suppliers' invoices in a half-arch file when several raps sound on the wooden door. It opens a crack and his ageing bartender sticks his half-bald head in. "Sir, there's a man outside. He says he wants to see you."

Kiattisak flicks his gaze up from the file to the bartender. "What about?" His voice sounds like a bullfrog's croak.

"He's looking for work."

Kiattisak arches his beetle eyebrows. "Is he young and handsome?"

"Yes."

"Alright, send him in." Kiattisak closes the file and pushes it aside.

The bartender pushes the door fully open with his palm and

moves away to allow a thirty-something-year-old man to step inside the room. Wearing a short-sleeved Hawaii style shirt, he has a strong jaw and big eyes.

"*Sawadee-kap!*" greets the visitor, garbed in a pink shirt and cream-coloured pants which compresses his butt tightly.

"Sit down." Kiattisak jerks his stubby chin in the direction of a chair across him, his eyes assessing his visitor. "What's your name?" He leans his huge frame back on his swivel chair and strokes his moustache with one hand.

The man grabs the back of the chair, pulls it out with a screech and sinks down on it. "My name's Panit Suparat." He crosses his legs at the knees and rests both hands on his lap. "I want to work here but only in the evenings. I sell *pad Thai* during the day."

"This is a gay bar. Any experience working in a gay bar?"

"No."

"So, why should I hire you?"

Panit straightens his posture. "I'm good with my mouth, my ass and my cock!" His voice is as steely as the expression on his face. "I can bring in more business for your bar!"

Kiattisak's eyes span wider to reveal a twinkle. "Ahh! I like your style, Panit!" He jabs a finger like Donald Trump in his *The Apprentice* but instead of saying "You're fired!" he snaps with gusto, "You're hired!"

Two nights later...

Lying on his stomach in the room of a love motel, Panit grimaces as the *farang*, twice his size and almost twice his age, enters him from the rear. *Oh Lord Buddha! My asshole's going to tear!*

An hour earlier, the *farang* had barfined him out of Hard Horny Bar after buying him several drinks. This is Panit's first night at work after selling *pad Thai* in the afternoon.

Arrrrrgh! Gritting his teeth, he feels the *farang*'s hip bone slapping repeatedly against his buttocks like a sledge hammer and his hands claw the bed sheet to withstand the pain. *Eeeeewwwww! This session is as painful as visiting a dentist!*

Several minutes pass. *Oh hell! I feel like shitting!* The next instant, against his will, Panit defecates.

A whack from a big hairy fist lands on the back of his head. *Thwack!* "You son-of-a-bitch! You've crapped on my dick!" A grubby hand grabs a bunch of his hair and yanks his head up, causing his neck to creak. "Don't you know you should empty your bowels before starting work?" hisses the *farang* in his ear, his hot breath almost making his skin shiver. "Next time, take laxatives, you understand?"

"I'm sorry, darling." Panit's voice almost cracks with strain. "This is my first day at work. I'll get toilet paper and clean up the mess. I'll also rinse the soiled parts of the bed sheet in the wash basin."

Six months later...

Chaiporn and his two younger sisters hear the ice-cream man's bell outside the house and run to the bathroom where Panit is taking a shower inside after having returned from Pattaya half-an-hour ago.

"*Phx!*" hollers Chaiporn outside the bathroom door. "We want to eat ice cream. The ice-cream man has stopped outside our neighbour's house."

"Ask *Mae* to buy for all of you," comes a muffled reply through the door. "Tell her to get the money from my wallet. It's inside my duffel bag."

"Yippee!" Chaiporn runs to the kitchen to seek out his mother.

Seconds later, Janjai rifles her husband's duffel bag in the bedroom. Through a jumble of sweat-stained clothes, she plucks out a pack of cigarettes and a matchbox. The label on the matchbox grabs her attention. *Hard Horny Bar? What's this doing here?* Casting the matchbox and packet of cigarettes back in the bag, she finds his wallet in a side pocket and opens it. A folded piece of paper is tucked in a card-holder compartment. She tugs the paper out, unfolds it and reads it. Her eyes span wider in alarm. *This is a laboratory test report with Panit's name on it. HIV test. Negative.* Huh? *STD. test. Negative.* Her forehead suddenly beaded with sweat, she returns the paper to its former place, takes out some money notes and slides the wallet back in the side pocket of the bag.

Janjai swallows her food and pushes her empty plate to the side. "Panit, what work are you doing in Pattaya?" Her lips thin along with her eyes.

"What do you mean? You already know, don't you?" Panit puts down his fork and spoon on the edge of his plate. "I sell *pad Thai* and I work as a night-shift cashier." The tone of his voice has a forced casualness to it.

In the centre of the table between them are platters with the dregs of vegetables and fried meat. Murmurs from a nearby bedroom reveal that the three kids have not fallen asleep.

"Is that the truth?"

A wispy sigh parts from his lips. "What are you implying?"

"I stumbled upon your HIV test report and a Hard Horny Bar matchbox in your bag this afternoon." Janjai locks gazes with

Panit, her brows in a scrunch. "Have you been visiting prostitutes in Pattaya?"

"Of course not!"

"Then why you need the HIV test?"

There is silence from Panit, who averts his wife's eyes.

"Come on, tell me the truth – a husband and wife should have no secrets from each other."

"It's – it's because I'm a male prostitute in Pattaya!" The words are spewed out like they were poison.

"What!" An eddy of stun whirls in Janjai's mind, paralyzing her for a moment. "But why?" Her tone of voice is as tight as the nerves in her neck

Panit's head slumps down out of shame. "Because I don't want you to become a bargirl! It's a lesser evil that I become a male prostitute!" Tears stream in rivulets down his cheeks as he lifts his gaze to meet his wife's, revealing a love for her so deep and raw.

Janjai reaches across the table for Panit's hand, gripping it tightly, his pain becoming her own.

Sitting across me in Hard Horney Bar on Jomtien Beach, Panit pulls out his mobile phone from his shirt pocket, taps its screen and shows it to me. "This is my son, Chaiporn."

"He looks like you." I take a sip of my beer. "How long will you continue to work here?"

Panit slips the handphone back in his shirt pocket. "When I recall his smile as a baby, I know I can find the perseverance to continue working in this line for as long as possible until he completes his education."

* * *

Seated on a stool with his back facing the bar counter, Jamie Henderson (not his real name), aged thirty-eight, scans the dance floor littered with bargirls and portly patrons gyrating to the beat of the rock-and-roll music. From the corner of one eye, to his far right, he spots the bulky form of Mummy Jantra approaching the bar. He climbs down from his stool, strides past four other patrons sitting in a line and stops at an arm's length away from the mamasan. Mummy is now leaning on the bar and jabbering something to the bartender, who nods assiduously.

When Mummy turns from the bar to walk away, Jamie addresses her, "Hi, Mummy! Can I talk to you for a while?"

Mummy's eyes span wider in surprise. "Why, Jamie, it's you!" A smile tugs at her thick lips, revealing dimples in her cherubic cheeks. "Sure, what's it regarding?"

"Your go-go dancer Araporn."

"She's off tonight but my other dancers are equally friendly."

"I know Araporn's off. But can I ask something about her?"

"What about?" Mummy squishes her hand-drawn eyebrows, and at that moment, the sound of piano keys rattling the tune of *Boogie Woogie Stomp* blasts from loud speakers. "Oh, that's my favourite music!" She jerks her head toward the dance floor. "Come, let's dance! We'll talk while dancing!"

Mummy takes a few steps to a spot on the dance floor and Jamie follows her. Her feet start to step and tap in a pattern, her massive breasts bouncing along with each move, while Jamie lifts his lanky legs repeatedly like a cat on a hot tin roof.

"Yes, Jamie," asks Mummy, inhaling and exhaling though her mouth, "what about Araporn?"

The groove of the music prompts Jamie to swing his arms. "Is she single or married?"

"Why don't you ask her yourself?"

Mummy and Jamie shuffle nearer and the mamasan stretches out her thick right arm.

"I have but I want you to confirm her answer." Jamie holds Mummy pudgy hand, their feet moving in slick action. "She's single, right?"

Jamie and Mummy switch places with hands clasped. "I can't disclose personal info about my staff." They lock gazes for a moment and release hands.

Jamie arches his brows. "I'll give you a fat tip later."

"Great!" Mummy casts a momentary glance at Jamie's moving feet shod in sneakers. "Why you want to know?"

"I think I'm falling in love with her."

"Araporn's single, never married."

"Any bad habits like gambling or drugs?"

Mummy shakes her head. "Nope." Several strands of stray hair fall over one eye.

"Any boyfriend?"

Mummy pushes the stray strands of hair away. "All her regular *farang* customers can be considered boyfriends."

"I mean Thai boyfriend?"

"Not that I know of." Mummy starts to pant, her breath coming in rasps. "She's devoted to her family in Udon Thani province, goes back on her off-days every month." She waves a hand at a passing bargirl who approaches her. "Okay, I gotta go!" says Mummy to Jamie and then she turns to the bargirl standing a few feet away. "Bussaba, dance with this gentleman, please!"

Mummy stops dancing and lumbers away, her forehead beaded with sweat.

A year later…
Jamie Henderson and his wife, Araporn, are sitting in the doctor's waiting room and browsing a magazine each when the receptionist leans to the window in her booth and calls, "Mr. and Mrs. Henderson, please go in."

The couple rises, toss their magazines on their empty chairs and enter the doctor's room. They sit across the thick-set, bull-necked doctor at a glass-topped desk.

Jamie nods. "So, doctor, why isn't my wife conceiving after almost one year of marriage?" He blinks his eyes in anticipation of the answer.

The doctor opens a folder file in front of him. "Mr. and Mrs. Henderson –" his stentorian voice sounds like the rumble of distant thunder " – based on the test results both of you are healthy to be parents." He tosses his gaze at Araporn. "Mrs. Henderson, the intrauterine ultrasound examination does not show any fibroid tumour or ovarian cyst. Hormonal levels are also normal." He leans forward in his chair and its springs creak under his massive weight. "May I know whether you've miscarried before?"

"Nope." Araporn gives a gentle shake of her head, her ponytail quivering with the motion.

The doctor flicks his gaze down on the paper in the folder and then up to Jamie. "Mr.Henderson, analysis of your semen does not show anything abnormal. Sperm count and sperm motility are normal." Deep in thought for a moment, he bites his lower lip. "Perhaps, the timing of copulation was not right." His eyes light up. "Mrs. Araporn Henderson, can you remember how many days was each of your menstrual cycle for the past three months? And the date of your last period. If you can give me the information, I can calculate your fertile period."

Ah, what the heck! That's not going to work! "Err, I'm not sure." *I'm on contraceptives discreetly! I don't wish to be a mother!* "Can I keep track and give you the information later?"

"Of course." The doctor leans back in his chair. "You can give me a call." He takes out a pen from his shirt pocket and starts to write on the paper in the folder. "In the meantime, I'll prescribe some fertility pills for you, madam."

"Doctor," says Jamie sitting up straight, "shall I continue to take the zinc supplement?"

"By all means do." The doctor nods. "Also, cut down on the beer!"

A month later...
Feeling his bowels cramping, Jamie gets up from his office desk and strides to the men's toilet. Contracting his asshole to contain the poop pressure, he enters a cubicle, unbuttons his pants and pulls down his briefs. Alas, before he can flip down the toilet seat, an imminent explosion of gooey black material spurs him to plunk his butt down on the ceramic bowl. He releases the devil's cut. *Damn! Must be food poisoning!* He remains in a half-squatting position for several seconds until the purge ends and washes up with a bum gun. *I better go see a doctor and take the day off.*

Two hours later, Jamie slides the key into the front door of his condominium, opens it and steps inside. Music is playing from the hi-fi set in the living room but there is nobody there. Kicking off his shoes, he pads across the living room to the dining room which adjoins the kitchen. *Odd. Araporn is not here either.*

Muffled thumping sounds like a headboard hitting a wall come from his bedroom. *Eh? What's that noise in the bedroom?* He moves to the bedroom and, without knocking, latches his hand on the door handle and opens the door.

His jaw goes slack. The metal legs of his four-poster bed are wobbling and the box springs in the mattress are squeaking like a rat being tortured. A naked Araporn is lying atop another woman and humping away as if riding a bucking bronco!

"Eeeeeeeek!" screams the other woman.

Araporn rolls away from her partner. "Oh shit!" She lays on her back next to her, her chest heaving, a dildo strapped to her crotch, her long hair in wild disarray. "Don't you have the courtesy to knock?" The smell of perfume from her body collides with the scowl on her face.

"Y-you're a lesbian!" Jamie feels like he has been punched in the gut.

"Sorry, darling – yes, I am." She gets off the bed and takes off her dildo. "That's why I don't want to be a mother!" She moves to the dresser, pulls out a drawer and keeps the dildo inside. "I've been on contraceptives."

Paralyzed to the spot by shock, Jamie tosses his gaze at Araporn's lover. "You're Pimchan!" A sick feeling throbs in his chest as the other woman rolls off the bed and starts to put on her clothes. "You're the go-go dancer in my wife's former bar!" *Hell, they were frequently dancing as a lesbian pair on stage and I thought it was an act. Never figured they're lesbians in real life.*

Pimchan and Araporn, now fully dressed, leave the bedroom with linked hands.

The telephone in Madam Buakai Wattapongsiri's (not her real

name) office rings and she picks up the receiver, holding it to one ear. "Hello? Buakai Property Consultants, Buakai Wattapongsiri speaking." She leans forward and places an elbow on the scuffed teak table. "How can I help you?"

"Hello, my name's Jamie Henderson. I am an expat in Pattaya. I wish to rent a fully furnished bungalow in the outskirt of the city for four months. My relatives from London are coming for a visit and I'm playing host." The voice sounds serious, earnest and full of remorse.

"How many rooms?" She removes her spectacles with one hand. "With or without swimming pool?" She twirls the spectacles between her thumb and forefinger.

"Three rooms are sufficient. Swimming pool is not necessary but a plus. More important is a high wall around the property and top-notch security. My relatives are very rich and very private people, so a bungalow without any neighbour in the vicinity will be perfect."

"Yes, Mr. Henderson, we've a vacation home for rent – three rooms, two bathrooms and a swimming pool at the back. It's near Lake Chak Nok, only six kilometres' drive to Jomtien Beach, has beautiful country views. The property has a security system and is surrounded by a metal palisade fencing almost ten feet high. When do you want to see it?"

"How about tomorrow?"

Buakai replaces her spectacles. "Sure, come to my office and we can go together." Her face glows with happiness.

Jamie spears a piece of chicken from a platter in the centre of the dining table with his fork. "Darling," he says, bringing the chicken to his mouth, "I've decided that we should go spend a week in a meditation centre." He starts to chew. "I feel that we should make efforts to repair our marriage – get away from the stress of modern life, find inner peace and return to the right path."

Araporn takes a sip of her lemongrass tea, eyeing him over the rim of her glass. "Are you referring to Boonkanjanaram Meditation Centre?" She puts the glass down on the table, her big brown eyes shining with loveliness in themselves and at the same time disdain for Jamie. *He's quite a weakling, not daring to quarrel with me over last week's incident.*

Jamie swallows his food. "No, there's a new one near Lake Chak Nok."

"You think meditation is going to change my sexuality?" Araporn's lips curl with contempt.

Jamie puts his fork and spoon down. "What I want is for us to spend quality time together, add a dose of Dharma teachings and meditation." He pushes his plate away and pulls out a tissue from a nearby box. "Then, see how things work out." He wipes his lips with the tissue paper. "Your love is important to me, so there's no harm in us trying, isn't it?" The tone of his voice is gentle.

Araporn smiles and bites her lip. "What if I have other plans?"

Avoiding Araporn's eyes, Jamie casts his gaze at the dregs of food on the platters. "Then you won't be getting your monthly allowance." His voice deepens to a serious level.

Wipers sweep the windscreen in arcs, clearing the splatter of raindrops. Hunched in the driver's seat, Jamie squints through the rain and sees the single-storey bungalow ahead. He flips the indicator, makes the right turn and drives up a short tarred road.

He stops outside a massive wrought iron gate and toots his horn. From a hut behind the wrought iron gate a man dashes out, performs a mock salute at Jamie and dashes inside again. The gate swings inward and Jamie drives up the concrete pathway, stopping his car under the porch.

In the front passenger seat, Araporn arches her delicate brows in question. "Is this the meditation centre?" Her brown eyes survey her surroundings with a puzzled gaze. "I don't see any signboard?"

"This place is still new—signs are not up yet." Jamie yanks the handbrake up, his heart hammering in his chest as hard as the rain on the porch roof. "Come, our meditation guru is waiting inside." He gets out of the car, walks to the boot and opens it. As Araporn steps out of the car, Jamie hefts two suitcases out, places them on the floor and slams the boot shut. The smell of freshly cut grass and mulch floating from the lawn on both sides of the house heightens his senses, and he takes a deep inhale.

The front door swings open as it is pulled from the inside and a tall middle-aged Thai woman with a sun-wrinkled face and a thick-set body steps out and moves to one side. "Good morning, Mr. Henderson," greets the woman in a warm voice, and then, shifting her voice from friendly to cold, she flicks her gaze at Araporn, the latter only standing up to the former's shoulder. "My name's Jamnong." Jamie and Araporn enter the house with Jamnong in tow and she closes the door behind her.

Inside the living room, as Araporn is casting a sweeping glance at the furniture, she hears the lock click. "What kind of place is this?" Her eyes span wider and she turns to face her husband. "Jamie, what're you up to? This is not a meditation centre!" Her wary voice brims with rage.

Jamnong stretches out beefy arms to take the suitcases from Jamie and starts to wheel them to the master bedroom.

"We'll be staying here for four months!" Jamie's gaze almost sears Araporn. "Jamnong will cook for us. She and my guard have instructions not to let you leave this place." A tic pulses in his jaw. "Jamnong's skilled in martial arts, so don't try to get physical with her."

"What!" Fingers of fear grip Araporn's heart, now throbbing like a raw wound. "Why're you keeping me here?"

"Remember what you said about having children before we married? You said you love kids! You've lied to me! I want you to keep your promise." He wags a finger in Araporn's face. "I want you to bear me a child!" Fire sparks in his eyes. "Once you're four months pregnant, we'll return to our condo. By that time, no doctor can perform an abortion on you. After the birth of our child, I'll be more than happy to divorce you."

"What makes you think you'll get custody of the child?"

"In the eyes of a divorce judge," says Jamie, edging up one corner of his mouth, "you think an ex-ago-go dancer-cum-lesbian with no future proper job is fit to be a single mother?"

Lying in bed, Jamnong closes her eyes but before sleep can envelope her, screams and hoarse grunts muffling from the adjacent master bedroom alert her. *Oh Lord Buddha, Jamie is committing marital rape again! This is the fifth consecutive night! The snake wine he has been consuming every evening after dinner must be effective!*

Now, repeated thuds of bed posts against the wall jar her ear drums. She turns her head sideways, pulls her fluffy pillow from under her head and places it over the side of her face, covering her ear. *Now I remember – Jamie has not bought the pregnancy self-test kit yet. Tomorrow, I better remind him.* A short while later, Jamnong, a widow, feels her crotch pulsing and throbbing, almost matching the rhythm of the thuds on the wall, as sexual fantasies grip her mind.

One month later…

Holding a plate piled with two pieces of toast with beefy arms, Jamnong – clad in pants and dress shirt – steps out of the kitchen and enters the dining room. "Jam or butter?" she asks Araporn, sitting at the table, as she puts the plate in front of the latter.

"Strawberry jam," replies Araporn in a cold tone, recalling yesterday's incident. *She's a tough bitch!* She grabs the coffee pot not far from her, fills up the cup in front of her and returns the pot to its former place.

Yesterday, after Jamie left for work, Araporn planned to go through Jamnong's pockets for the house keys so she sneaked up from behind her in an attempt to tie her hands with the power cord of a hair dryer. However, Jamnong proved to be too strong and shoved her away like a rag doll.

Araporn lifts the cup to her lips but before she can drink the coffee, a wave of nausea rises from her throat, and she bends forward retching, her hand flying to her mouth. *Dammit! It's too late to try to escape!*

At that moment, Jamnong appears at Araporn's side with a jar of jam in one hand. "Aha! Looks like morning sickness!" She puts the jar on the table. "I'll put a glass on the sink counter in your bathroom afterward. I want you to pee in it so that I can do a pregnancy test." She returns to the kitchen.

Another two months later...

Jamie's handphone lying on the office desk buzzes and the caller I.D. shows Jamnong. He picks it up and taps "Answer" on the screen.

He holds his moby to his ear. "Yes, Jamnong?"

"Sir, your wife has locked herself in the bedroom. She didn't come out for breakfast. An hour ago, I knocked on the door to ask her to take lunch. She shouted obscenities at me. Now, suddenly, it's very quiet inside." Her voice brims with concern. "I'm wondering what she's up to inside the room. What can I do?"

"I'll come back now!" Jamie pulls out a left-hand drawer. "Ask the guard to open the gate ready for me." He grabs his car keys, slams the drawer shut and takes quick steps to his office door.

One-and-a-half-hours later, Jamie swerves his car into the front porch, screeching its tyres as it comes to a stop.

Jamnong is waiting for him at the front doorway and he leaps out of the car and dashes inside the house. They move with wide strides to the door of the master bedroom.

"Araporn, open the door!" Cheeks flaming hot, Jamie stands with fists hanging at his side. *I hope she's not so foolish as to attempt suicide!* "What're you doing inside? Come out for your lunch!" *But I doubt she's that brave.*

There is no reply and the silence causes Jamie's veins to pulse with worry. "Araporn, darling," he says, trying a soft approach. "As you're going to be the mother of my child, I love and cherish you. Please come out now for your lunch. Starving yourself will also starve the baby."

Again, there is no reply.

Jamie locks his gaze with Jamnong for a moment. "We've no choice but to force open the door!" His tone of voice is tight as muscles quiver in his jaw. "Let's charge at it together with our shoulders!" He pauses and takes a deep inhale. "Ready?" The duo takes two steps backward and crouch American-football style. "Now!" Like raging bulls, they lurch forward. Upon impact, a loud thud echoes in the house and pieces of wood tears and splinters from the door frame. The door comes off its hinges and falls with a clatter to the floor. Jamie comes to running stop inside the bedroom while Jamnong loses her balance and falls down face first.

Araporn is leaning against the headboard of the bed, her eyes gazing at the ceiling, her knees raised. Garbed in a cotton pink top, she is naked from the waist down, and the bed beneath her buttocks is covered with a circle of dark blood.

Lips twisted in a sinister grin, Araporn shoots Jamie a piercing glare. "I've aborted the two-month-old foetus!" She points to splodges of grayish material splattered on the bed between her thighs and a hysterical laugh erupts from her lips.

Jamie recoils in horror, bile rising in his throat, eyes spanning wider. "Huh? How?"

Araporn holds up a straight length of wire with a bloodied curve at one end. "With this! It's a former wire clothes hanger!" She hikes her chin in defiance, eyes glittering like pieces of broken glass. "You can't force me to do what I don't want to!"

Jamie stares open-mouthed at her, her guts of steel chilling him to the bone.

At that moment, Jamnong gets up and casts her gaze at the scene on the bed. "Eeeeeeeeek!" she screams and faints, crumpling into a pile beside the bed.

Mummy Jantra lifts up a glass of tequila to her ruby lips with a pudgy hand, upends it, draining it dry. "Was my story interesting?" Her thick lips part with a sharp exhale as she slams the glass down on the steel table.

"Of course!" I quirk one side of my mouth up in a half smile.

Mummy grins. "Hi-five!" Her grin blossoms into a smile as she raises her right palm in my direction. Sweet thunderation! My mouth goes slack. The word "Big Tip" is written on her palm using a black ballpoint pen. I slap her palm with my own, fumble in my trouser pocket for my wallet and tug it out.

I slip out a few money notes from my wallet. "Is Araporn back here as go-go dancer?" I stuff them into the metal bin in the centre of the table.

"Nope," says Mummy, picking up the money notes, "after her self-abortion, she returned to her home village to visit her parents." She stuffs the notes in her cleavage peeking out from a tight sequined top. "She never returned because she died of septicemia. She was too late in seeking medical attention."

Jesus Christ! My jaw drops a second time.

6

Bangkok:
Lesser-known Little Tokyo

Located only five hundred metres from Patpong Night Market, Thaniya Road and a few adjacent alleys are packed with sake bars, nightclubs, ago-go bars, member-only clubs, karaoke bars, massage parlours, ramen joints and sushi restaurants. Sporting signs in both *hiragana* (or Japanese characters) and English, they cater mainly to Japanese expats and Japanese tourists.

My tuk-tuk drops me at Thaniya Plaza at Silom Road, which is the best-known landmark for the Thaniya Road area. The plaza stands adjacent to Sala Daeng BTS Station and walking across Silom Road will bring me to Thaniya Road which stretches northward to end perpendicular to Surawong Road. But first, I tour Thaniya Plaza whose main entrance is flanked by massive twin pillars on both sides. The first floor is dominated by stores selling clothes and golf equipment. Second floor sees more golf stores, three Japanese restaurants and a few clothing stores. Golf stores again dominate the third floor and two Japanese restaurants are found here. On the fourth floor is housed a doctor's clinic, a dental clinic, a beauty centre and a motley collection of stores. Since I am not a golfer, my tour ends quickly and I proceed to Thaniya Road.

Decorated with pulsing neon lights and flashy advertisement light boxes, the drag is lined with eateries and nightspots of all kinds. A left building ahead houses several joints as indicated by a sorority of promotional girls standing on its front sidewalk. While walking, my attention is yanked to the other side of the road by hard-sell girls sitting on plastic stools placed at the roadside. When I refocus my attention ahead, I am in front of Sekushi Club (not its real name).

"*Hansamuna otoko, kangei no kana,*" hollers a lass wearing a red tube top, a mini-skirt and five-inch heels. Her three other companions pay no attention me as their gazes continue to scour the foot traffic on the roadside.

I stand at an arm's length away from her. "I'm not Japanese, can I enter?"

"Oh, I'm sorry, I thought you're Japanese. Actually, this club is for Japanese only." She takes a step backward and points to one of four LED advertisement panels on the façade wall of the building. "You can go up Hottogaru Bar on the third floor. Non-Japanese are welcome there."

I toss my gaze to two other LED advertisement panels on the wall. "What about Sasaki KTV on the second floor and Nagasaki Bar & Grill on the fourth floor?"

"No, they're also exclusive to Japanese."

Going up to the third floor sounds like a hassle to me so I continue to traipse ahead. After passing stores and restaurants, I'm nearing Tenshi Ago-Go Bar (not its real name) which has a signage flashing on and off above its tinted glass-door. One of two PR girls – both wearing rabbit-ear hair bands – steps forward and flashes me a smile. "*Ba e yokoso!*"

"Can a non-Japanese enter this bar?"

"Of course! Welcome! Lots of girls inside!" Her heels click on the sidewalk as she moves towards the glass door. "I'll take you to your table." She pushes the glass door open and stands with her back pressed against it, allowing me to enter. We step into a small lobby and, now, she takes longer strides than me so as to be ahead of me. We round a *shoji* screen with a picture of Mt. Fuji and enter a hall filled with oval-shaped tables and leather lounge chairs. While I am being blasted by karaoke singing by a middle-aged Japanese guy – who looks like a salaryman – standing on a stage, the PR girl sits me at a table with two leather lounge chairs.

A mamasan dressed in a kimono sashays to me and hands me a menu. Her hair is held up by two traditional Japanese-style hair pins made of lacquered wood. "Our beaaaautiful ago-go girls are upstairs," she says, turning her head in the direction of a staircase at one end of the hall. I order *umeshu* or plum wine, return the menu to her and survey my surroundings. Great balls of fire! On the ceiling is suspended a canopy of cherry blossom lights. It's beautiful. Almost all tables are taken up with Japanese patrons – a few wearing blazers – ranging from three to six in number at a table, and a standing bar is set parallel to one wall.

My drink arrives which I pay for immediately and I observe the goings-on. By now, the salaryman has finished singing to loud applause from a particular table. I sip my *umeshu* and its sweetness coaxes my tongue to lick my upper palate. Moments later, I see the back of a fat Japanese bloke who's lumbering up the three steps to the stage with his shapely Thai hostess following behind. When he turns around to face the patrons, my jaw goes slack! Glassy-eyed, he is wearing a dark necktie around his forehead! The blade of the necktie is dangling down one side of his red face.

Staring at a LED monitor, the duo starts to sing. Expecting them to sing a Japanese song, I am jerked upright in my seat by surprise as they belt out *You Don't Have to Be a Star*, popularized by Marilyn McCoo and Bill Davis Junior. However, the inebriated roly-poly sings out of tune and with slurred pronunciation which drives me to chug the contents of my glass empty so I can leave. I rise from my seat and wend my way around tables to head upstairs. As I'm sauntering past a table, I overhear a buxom hostess say to her Japanese companion, "Feel my boobs, darling!" When he cups one breast, she utters, "No silicon! Natural! Come, want to barfine me out?"

At the staircase landing, I push open a clear glass door to enter a hall brightly lit in orange hues. Immediately inside the door sits a burly bouncer on a high-back stool. Two long walls of the hall are fitted with banquettes, and between them stands a long stage with shiny chrome poles. Garbed in bikinis, eight girls are gyrating their bodies suggestively to the latest music. All the twenty over men sitting on the banquettes are ogling at them. From nowhere, the same mamasan accosts me and steps into my private space. She raises herself on her soles, puts one hand to my ear and says above the music, "You can ask any girl to sit on your lap or barfine her out." I nod in understanding and settle down in a gap between a glassy-eyed, lanky Japanese, probably in his mid-thirties, and a scrawny guy wearing a toothbrush moustache.

The fast-tempo music ends and is replaced by sexy strains from a saxophone. Now, the dancers start to perform upper body undulations, making their stomach muscles move in ripples. My gaze snaps sideways to the lanky Japanese beside me as he stands up and staggers to the stage near a long-haired dancer. She moves to the edge of the stage, turns her big butt to face him and bends forward. Now, she teases him by turning her butt slowly in a circle. Suddenly, the lanky Japanese grabs the dancer's rump with both hands, bends forward and bites her on the butt! My mouth slacks open.

"Owwww!" The long-haired dancer jerks upright and rubs the spot where she was bitten, while the other girls stare wide-eyed at the inebriated Dracula but continue to dance. The gorilla-faced bouncer springs to his feet and strides towards the culprit, now wearing a sheepish expression.

"So solly! So solly!" The lanky Japanese bows slightly to the dancer. "I was carried away by your sexy dancing." He fishes out his wallet. "I give big tip as compensation." He takes out some money notes. "Come, I put money under your bikini." The dancer steps forward and he slips them under the elastic of her bikini. "I will barfine you out shortly." He returns to his former spot on the banquette.

With the situation diffused, the bouncer returns to his high-back stool and I call it a night.

* * *

It's 2 a.m. in Udayadit Casino (not its real name) in the Cambodian town of Poipet on the Thailand-Cambodia border, and the gaming hall is near-deserted. Thirty-year-old Ritthirong, a bartender from Bangkok, settles down at the blackjack table and tosses a bunch of US dollar notes on the table. "Ten forty-dollar chips, please." He holds the amulet hanging from his neck and blows at it, hoping the gesture will give him good luck.

Earlier in the afternoon, Ritthirong had his wallet emptied by the roulette wheel and slot machines, and a Cambodian loan shark approached him with an offer. "The loan can be approved very quickly. We just need details of your home address and working place in Bangkok and their phone numbers. After our associates in Bangkok verify the information, we'll give you the loan amount in cash." A deal was sealed at an interest rate of twenty percent per day for a four-figure loan in US dollars.

Presently, after counting the notes, the dealer – a twenty-something lass – picks up ten chips from an acrylic rack, puts them on the table and pushes them to Ritthirong. "Here you are, sir." She pauses. "Ready?" Her dark-brown eyes twinkle with anticipation.

Ritthirong, the sole gambler at the table, rubs his hands and places two chips in the betting circle. From a dealing shoe sitting at her left, the dealer slides two cards to him and opens them. Ritthirong's eyes span wider and his breath hitches. *Ten of diamonds and three of clubs! Sheesh! Not a good start!*

The dealer opens her first card which shows a seven of diamonds, while the other card remains faced down. Though wearing heavy make-up, her expression is stony.

Pulse staggering, Ritthirong wriggles two fingers of his right hand and utters, "Hit!"

The dealer deals another card to Ritthirong and opens it to reveal a seven of hearts.

Whoopee! Twenty! A grin flickers on his lips.

The dealer opens her second card. It's a four of clubs. Her neck muscle twitters. She continues to deal. Her third card is a three of hearts, and her fourth card is an eight of spade. Bust! Smiling, she rewards Ritthirong with four chips and the game continues.

During the next one hour, however, Lady Luck abandons Ritthirong, and he walks away from the blackjack table with his face as black at the cloudy night outside. He has been wiped clean, and tomorrow, when he checks out of his hotel to take a bus back to Bangkok, his credit card will be maxed out to its limit.

The noise of his two pre-school children playing in the living room reaches Ritthirong as he approaches his flat in Khlong Toei, Bangkok. He opens the iron grille door with a twist of his key and enters the small living room.

His children patter to the kitchen, shouting, "*Mae, Phx* is back!"

The aroma of spices floating from the kitchen tickles Ritthirong's nostrils as he steps out of his sneakers and kicks them to one side. He walks straight to his bedroom. As he is taking off his shirt, his wife Prija enters the bedroom and closes the door behind her. "*Thirak* [darling], how did things turn out at the casino?" She is wearing an apron and her hair is tied up in a ponytail.

"I-I lost everything." His voice is rusty, like he's sick with a cold.

"What! I told you not to go but you wouldn't listen!" Her breath catches in her throat, colliding with anger, and, a moment later, she draws in a calming breath. "While you were away, someone phoned the fixed line for you. I told him you were out of town. He refused to give me his name and hung up. Then shortly, a stocky man came to look for you. I told him the same thing. Odd. Again, he refused to identify himself, said he's a good friend of yours. Then he left. Who are these people?"

"They're probably from the money-lending syndicate, verifying the information I've given them when I applied for a loan."

Prija cocks her head. "So, what about my allowance for this month?"

"Didn't you hear me? I already told you I lost everything, including – " the muscles in his throat struggle to form the words " – the loan!" He runs a shaky hand through his hair. "Withdraw from your savings account first. Let me think of something and I'll give the allowance to you later." His body goes slack as he exhales in despair. "Now, please leave me alone to change and bathe." His stomach cramps.

A month later...

The hall of Kabuki KTV Bar (not its real name) at Thaniya Road is still shrouded in a veil of semi-darkness as it has not opened for business. In its back section, Mummy Phitsamai hunches over a tiny desk in her cubicle. As she removes the previous night's receipts for barfines and lady's drinks one by one from a spike holder, she tallies their amounts by tapping the keys of an electronic calculator with her other hand. While in the midst of performing this task, a knock sounds on the door of her cubicle. "Yes? Come in." She throws her gaze from her desk to the door, which swings inward.

Wearing a dark vest, Ritthirong is standing in the doorway. "Good afternoon, Mummy, sorry to bother you, but I've a personal problem." He bows slightly. "Can I discuss it with you?" He has a weak chin, sunken cheeks and a large nose.

"Sure." Mummy Phitsamai motions her hand towards one of two chairs across her desk.

Ritthirong settles down on the low-backed chair and sits straight like a ramrod. His eyes look tired and are spidered in red.

Dark eyebrows drawn in a curve lift upward as the mamasan hikes her chin. "Yes? What's your problem?"

"It's like this, Mummy." Ritthirong harrumphs to clear his

throat. "I lost money speculating on the stock market last month. Now I need to settle several bills urgently. Can you give me a loan?"

"How much do you want to borrow?"

"Eighty thousand."

"What! That's a big sum!" The air in Mummy Phitsamai's chest hitches. "What stocks did you speculate on?"

"That's not important, is it? I just need the money." His eyes entreat hers.

"Come on, don't lie." Mummy's eyes sear him like acid as she levels a stiff finger in Pitthitong's direction. "From what I heard from my girls, you like to gamble! So, where did you go to this time? Genting Highlands or Poipet?" She leans back on the chair. "Sorry, I don't believe in paddling another person's boat, especially if it's leaking because of gambling." She rests her elbows on the arms of the chair and steeples her hands. "Why don't you ask for an advance from Pete?"

"I did, but he said no." His tone of voice is dry.

"Then I can't help you."

"Mummy, this time I'm in deeper shit than before." His body starts to quiver in short heaves. "I-I'm involved with a ruthless loan shark in Poipet who has connections with the Bangkok mafia. I need the money urgently." His eyes are glazed with hope. "I understand you're on friendly terms with several of our regular customers. A few of them have super-fat wallets. Can you approach them on my behalf?"

"Why should any of them want to help you?"

Ritthirong scrubs his hand over his head and the crease in his frown deepens. "That's a good question. Err – but, anyway, can you at least try?" He pauses for impact. "It's because you're like an elder sister to me that I venture to ask this favour." He struggles to form the words which seem fused to his tongue. "Please...please help me."

One corner of Mummy Phitsamai's mouth curls in sympathy mixed with scorn. "Alright, I'll sound them out."

Mummy Phitsamai steps to the wall-mounted magazine rack and takes out the current edition of *Nikkan Bankoku Shinbun*. She enters the Ume KTV Suite where Takamizu Takashi (not his real name), CEO of a Japanese-Thai joint-venture manufacturing company, is lounging on a plush velvet settee. His thin frame is enveloped in a long-sleeved shirt with the sleeves rolled up three turns and his brown slacks are matched with sneakers of the same colour. A sake decanter and a porcelain cup are set in front of him. The fragrance of lavender from an air-freshener has undressed the room of stale cigarette smoke, and a romantic Japanese melody drifting in the air caresses him like a plume.

"Good evening, Takashi-san." *I hope he's in a good mood tonight.* "Here's a newspaper for you to read while you wait for your business associates." She passes the folded newspaper to him who places it on his lap. In the reflection of the mirror section of one wall, Mummy sees a good-looking man in his forties, with hair thinning at the temples. Since his posting to Bangkok two years ago, Takashi-san has been coming here once every week.

Before Takashi-san can open the newspaper, Mummy says, "Excuse me, can I trouble you regarding something?" A smile wheedles it way to the corners of her lips as she stands in front of him, head slightly bowed.

"Sure." His eyes flick up to meet hers.

Mummy moves to sink into a padded chair diagonally across him. "You know our bartender, don't you?" She leans forward and pours sake from a decanter into a porcelain cup. "Please." She nudges the cup forward slightly.

"Of course, I've spoken with Ritthirong many times before. He's quite creative with cocktails."

Mummy sits up straight. "I know his trouble doesn't concern you but he needs help desperately."

Takashi-san cocks a curious look at her. "What kind of help?"

"He needs a loan urgently, and he has asked me to convey his request to you."

"How did he get in financial woe?"

"Gambling debt."

Takashi-san takes a sip of his sake, savouring it with a dreamy roll of his eyes. "Oh? Is he a compulsive gambler?"

"I'm afraid so. A loan shark has been harassing him."

"Oh, no." Takashi-san crimps his brows in apparent concern. "What amount is he looking at?"

"Eighty thousand baht."

"There are three kinds of people you don't help by lending them money." A noisy sigh of apparent disgust rolls from his lips. "A drug addict, an alcoholic and a compulsive gambler. They'll spend the loan on their vices."

Mummy Phitsamai beams him an endearing smile, her penciled eyebrows arched in appeal. "Please...after all, we've known each other two years."

"Alright, let me talk to him."

Takashi-san's approachable gaze warms Mummy's cheeks. "Sure, I'll get him." She rises and leaves the karaoke room.

A few minutes later, Ritthirong is sitting across the coffee table opposite Takashi-san. The bartender is garbed in his usual black vest and a white short-sleeved shirt. Mummy Phitsamai is settled on her former seat and gazing at the porcelain sake decanter on the coffee table.

Takashi-san pins his gaze on Ritthirong face for a moment. "I understand from Mummy you want a loan of eighty thousand. To get a loan shark off your back, right?"

Excitement edges Ritthirong's voice. "Yes, sir."

Takashi-san crosses his legs at the ankles. "But how do you intend to repay it?" He leans back on the settee and folds his arms over his chest.

"I'll take a second part-time job."

"Doing what?" Takashi-san suddenly sits upright. "What other marketable skills do you have? And don't you need to sleep?" The tone of his voice is as sour as the plum-flavoured sweets in the glass bowl sitting in the centre of the coffee table.

"Err, I –" Ritthirong's lips part to answer but the quiver of his chin stops his words.

Silence settles in the room like a morning mist for several seconds.

"You're married, aren't you?"

"Yes, I am."

"How old is your wife?"

"Twenty-eight, and we have two kids – five and six years old this year."

"You love your wife very much?"

"Of course, sir. I'm a devoted family man."

"Tell you what. I won't lend you eighty thousand but I'll do better than that." Takashi-san hikes his chin and a sinister-looking smile hovers at the edges of his lips. "I'll give it to you. However, there is one condition."

"Oh? What?"

"Your wife has to spend one night with me! In a hotel, of course." The tone of his voice is emotionless, bordering on ruthlessness.

Eyes widened, Mummy Phitsamai snaps her gaze at Takashi-san.

Heat invades Ritthirong's cheeks. "What! You can't be serious?" His mouth gapes in shock. *If you weren't our patron, I'd clobber you right now!*

"I'm serious." Takashi-san's small eyes sparkle like broken jagged glass. "Talk to your wife, please." He pulls out his wallet from his back pocket and takes out a card. "Here's my name card. You can call my mobile once you and she have made a decision." He slips the card on the coffee table in front of Ritthirong.

Mummy stares at Ritthirong, his face a painful study of a man in love with his wife – yet mingling with desperation, hurt and guilt. As if in a trance, he lapses into a faraway stare as Takashi-san's offer apparently runs riot in his head.

Two nights later...

Pete, the Aussie bar manager, saunters into the men's L-shaped toilet, and the stink of ammonia stings his nostrils. Stepping past several cubicles, he heads for a row of urinals lining the shorter wall perpendicular to the long wall. He stops at the first urinal, unzips his fly and starts to pee. Amidst the dribble of his piss, he hears muffled sobbing emanating from one of the cubicles. Moments later, he zips his fly and goes to the sink to wash his hands. By now, the sobbing has stopped.

Stepping to the row of cubicles, Pete pushes the door of every cubicle inward one by one. At a certain cubicle, the door is locked. He remains standing and waits, and shortly, he hears sobbing again. "Hello! Who's inside?" He raps his knuckles on the door. "Are you alright?" His voice reeks of concern.

"Go away!"

Holy cow! It's our bartender! "Ritthirong, it's me, Pete! What's the matter? Open the door!"

The door swings inward to reveal Ritthirong sitting on the toilet lid with his back slumped against the cistern. His hands are hanging down his sides and ragged breaths are coming in heaves from his chest. His eyes are rimmed with tears and his face is twisted with anguish.

Eyes spanned wider in shock, Pete steps inside and places a hand on Ritthirong's shoulder. "What's wrong with you?"

Ritthirong scrubs his face with one hand.

"Hey, are you high on drugs?"

Ritthirong shakes his head. "No." The tone of his voice brims with a twang.

"Go wash your face. The club's opening in fifteen minutes' time. You better go to your work station."

"I – I can't – "

Pete ponders for a moment and draws in an inhale. "Alright, take this evening off." His blustery exhale comes with a shake of his head. "But I've to deduct one day from your annual leave. And I want an explanation from you tomorrow, you hear."

Throwing a lingering gaze at Ritthirong, Pete strides away from the loo, and in the corridor outside his room, he bumps into Mummy Phitsamai. "Mummy, just now I caught Ritthirong crying like a baby in the toilet." Furrows form between his blond thick eyebrows. "Do you know what's wrong with him?"

Mummy moves a step closer to Pete and half-whispers in a voice pregnant with scorn, "He just sent his wife to a hotel to have sex with another man."

"What!" Saliva sputters from Pete's mouth and his jaw sags. "What's the story?"

Meanwhile, in a luxury hotel, half a kilometre away, a shiny lift glides like a breeze to a stop and Prija steps out into the carpeted corridor. She has on a strapless halter top which reveals the sexy curve of her breasts. Wedges peep from under the hem of her jeans as she saunters to search for a particular room number. She finds it, stops and rings the door bell. A few moments later, the door is yanked open from the inside. A Japanese man dressed in a short-sleeved shirt is standing in the doorway, his hand on the doorknob.

"Mr. Takashi?" Prija's voice is as tight as the nerves in her body.

"Yes, I am." His nod comes with a warm smile. "You must be Prija?" He extends a hand, and they shake, the warmth of his palm swallowing the whole of her hand. She pulls away, ignoring the butterflies in her stomach, and he steps aside. "Please come in."

Prija moves into the spacious room, stops a few feet away from him and steps out of her wedges. Takashi motions with his hand towards one of two chairs at the far end of the room. "Come, let's sit down over there."

She saunters on bare feet to the chair, settles down and folds her legs under its edge. Takashi closes the door, locks it and shuffles in room slippers to sit in the other chair opposite her.

Resting his hands on his knees which are kept apart, he steers his gaze from her face down to her form-fitting halter top that flaunts her endowment. A big bulge in Takashi's crotch yanks Prija's attention downward and her breath hitches along with her pulse. *Oh Lord Buddha! He's already having a hard-on!*

"Your husband told you my condition?" His voice is stoic.

Prija flicks her eyes upward from under long curly lashes. "Yes." She draws in a stabilizing breath, heart stuttering at the intensity in his eyes.

"Where is he now?"

"Working at the nightclub."

"How's your marriage?"

"Can be better if it were not for his gambling habit."

"Now, compulsive gamblers must be taught a painful lesson so that they can reform." His lips clamp into a straight line for a moment. "So when your husband came to me for a loan, I wanted to punish him with an unforgettable lesson. That's why I told him you need to spend a night with me." He shifts a hip and pushes one hand deep into a side pocket. "This envelope contains eighty thousand baht," he says, wrenching out a thick brown package. He sits straight again and holds the envelope in his hands. "I'm going back to my condo now. But, I'd like you to stay the night here. Just play your role to teach him a lesson by going back the next morning. Hopefully, tonight's agonizing memory will make him change his ways."

"We are not going to have sex?"

"No, as I said, I'm going home now. But let this be our secret." He puts the envelope on the writing desk. "Prija, I may go to Kabuki Bar to book bargirls out but at the same time I have scruples. Like you, I'm also a Buddhist and I believe in karma.

So I don't use money to extort sex from a woman who's unlucky to be married to a compulsive gambler." He points with an open palm at the envelope. "Please take the money. There're so strings attached."

"Oh, Mr. Takamizu Takashi!" Her voice effuses joy. "Thank you!" She gets off the chair, stands with both legs closed together and executes a deep *wai*. "Thank you so much!" A deep flush of comfort scorches her rouged cheeks and burns all the way up to her scalp.

I lift my cup of sake, bring it to my mouth and upend it. "How did you know that Takashi did not have sex with her?" I put the cup down on the table.

"Two days later, Prija called me." Mummy Phitsamai takes the decanter and refills my cup. "We met at a nearby café, and she asked me to pass a present to Takashi-san." She clunks the decanter down on the table. "Prija explained what happened in the hotel room that night. Later, when I asked Takashi-san, he corroborated her story."

I flick my gaze to the man behind the bar. "That guy's Ritthirong?"

"No, that's not him, he's a new guy. A month after the incident, Ritthirong resigned out of shame. He knew that behind his back everybody in the bar was condemning him for having sold his wife."

7

Bangkok:
Days of Wine and Roses

Clad in white overalls, the pharmacist snaps her gaze from the computer screen to the glass door as it swings inward, causing the bell above it to ring. In steps a slender woman of medium height wearing a high-collar sheath dress. She has a narrow face and angular bones and eyes set wide apart. *It's Patcharapa. Wow! Today's dress flaunts her curvy figure well.* Patcharapa moves to the counter where the pharmacist is seated on a high stool, the latter's lips upturned in a smile. "Hello, what do you need this time?" She pauses and her smile turns into a grin. "The latest glow-in-the-dark condoms have arrived!" *Her clients love these novelty condoms.*

Standing across the counter, Patcharapa shakes her head. "I need something to help me kick my smoking habit."

"Want to try nicotine patch?" *Odd, why is she trying to quit?* The pharmacist climbs down from the high stool, turns and slides open the glass door of a cupboard behind her. *Maybe she's leaving the profession.*

Patcharapa rests an arm on the counter. "Apart from that, what other products do you have?" She shifts her weight to one foot, shod in kitten heel.

The pharmacist takes out a small packet from one of the

shelves. "Drugs like Zyban and Chantix can relieve nicotine withdrawal symptoms." She turns to face Patcharapa. "I don't stock them but if you can give me a prescription, I can order them for you." She hands the small packet to Patcharapa. "Here's the nicotine patch."

Patcharapa reads the product information on the package and flicks her gaze up to the pharmacist. "Can I take a shower while wearing a patch?"

"Of course."

"Great! Give me two boxes, please." She opens her handbag. "How much do I owe you?" She takes out some money notes. "By the way, I'll be leaving Bangkok to a faraway place soon."

Dr. Lumpoon (not his real name) looks up from a patient's card and leans forward on his chair. "Yes, Miss Patcharapa Uraiwan, how can I help you?"

"I want to have my tattoos removed." Patcharapa clasps her hands together. "What procedure do you use?" She rests them on her lap.

"Can be done either by surgery or laser." Dr. Lumpoon adjusts his half-framed spectacles. "Most of my patients prefer laser. It's relatively painless, leaves no scar and recovery time is usually shorter compared to surgery." He sucks in an inhale and releases it. "First, a local anesthetic will be applied to the area. Then a laser is applied to the tattoo which breaks down the pigments of the tattoo ink. The fragments are carried away by the body's immune system."

Patcharapa blinks. "Cost?"

"Total cost depends on the number of sessions required. That depends on the tattoo's size, colour and type of ink used.

Each session costs four thousand baht. But we're using the latest technology – the Picosecond laser which gives very effective results. If you've been asking around, you may find other dermatologists quoting you cheaper rates than us but they're still using the old Q-Switch laser."

"I see." Patcharapa unclasps her hands and rests them on the arms of the chair. "Perhaps you can give me an estimated cost after I show you my tattoos?"

"Of course."

Two months later...

Fifty-year-old Oscar Martin (a pseudonym) and twenty-five-year-old Patcharapa Uraiwan (not her real name) are sitting on a bench in the international departure lounge of Don Mueang International Airport in Bangkok. They are waiting to board a Thai Airways flight to Sydney.

"Are you excited, darling?" Oscar holds Patcharapa's hand resting on her lap. "We'll be husband and wife in a week's time!" He has on a short-sleeved checked shirt and black jeans.

"Not only excited, but nervous." Patcharapa turns her hand upward to grasp his fingers. "I hope I don't get air sickness; I also hope your family can accept me." Her anxious eyes cast a glance at the plasma screens displaying arrival and departure times on one wall.

Beer-bellied Oscar, who works as a production manager of a fruit cannery, hails from Bathurst, 200 km west of Sydney. Widowed three years ago, he has a son named Lucas, aged twenty-three, who lives with him and a married older daughter, Linda, who lives separately in Bathurst. Oscar met Pat (short for Patcharapa), an ago-go dancer of Nana Plaza, when he first visited

Bangkok two years ago and had been making regular visits ever since. Their long-distance romance culminated in a traditional marriage ceremony in her home village in Isaan a fortnight ago.

"Pooey!" Oscar snaps his chin up. "Who's to know of your background?" He releases her hand and smoothes the back of her head. "Just mind your Ps and Qs when you're in your new home."

Patcharapa tosses a sideward gaze at Oscar. "Ps and Qs?" Her cheeks warm as his gaze fuses to hers. "What's that?"

"Means mind your behaviour."

At Bathurst Railway Station, Lucas is waiting for his father and his future step-mother in the arrival platform. Togged up in baggy jeans, he squints at the milling crowd coming through the gates, trying to spot his father.

Oscar waves his hand. "Hey, Lucas, over here!"

A reedy man peering through thick spectacles approaches the couple. "How was the journey, Dad?"

"Son, this is Patcharapa Uraiwan – just call her Pat." Oscar turns to Pat. "My only son, Lucas. He works as a bookkeeper in a mining company."

"How do you do?" Pat extends her hand and Lucas pumps it briefly. *Oh Lord Buddha, his son is severely short-sighted. His spectacles are so thick.*

Lucas reaches out for the handle of Pat's roller luggage bag. "Can I take your luggage? My Ford Ranger is parked quite far away."

One month later...

Linda takes a sip of avocado juice and puts the glass down on the coffee table. She takes a plate of fruit slices from the coffee table and places it on her lap. "How's your keratoconus?" she asks Lucas. Linda spears a piece of pawpaw with a tiny plastic fork and starts to eat.

Sitting across her, Lucas is crunching sweet potato chips. "I'm getting custom-made soft contact lenses soon. They're called KeraSoft and are made by Bausch & Lomb. The eye doctor said it will help to correct the astigmatism greatly."

"That's good news." Linda flicks her gaze from her brother to Pat, sitting on a settee and chit-chatting with a few women at the far end of the hall. "What do you think of our step-mother?"

"She's adjusting well to life here." Lucas licks his lips. "I simply love her Thai dishes."

In the big hall, a white-linen-covered buffet table is set against one wall and is crammed with bottles of wine and vodka and platters of sweet-potato chips, bruschettas, quiches, tiny honey cakes, fruit slices, lamb chops and steaks. Holding wine glasses in their hands, four men are gathered in a corner and discussing the latest community news. In the back patio, Oscar is brushing olive oil on several pieces of steaks sizzling on a charcoal BBQ pit. His son-in-law is spearing chicken wings on metal skewers. Nearby, a kookaburra sitting on a gum tree is releasing a thrilling laugh.

Linda leans forward and takes her glass of avocado juice. "Any idea how Dad met her?" She takes a gentle sip.

"Dad said she was a cashier in a twenty-four-hour convenience store. His hotel was just nearby, and he went to the store to buy a few things. It was love at first sight, he said."

Oscar enters the hall with a platter of steaks and sets it on the buffet table. "More steaks are ready, everybody!" he announces. "Come, let's liven the party with some music." He moves to a CD player, taps a switch and returns to the back patio.

Fast-tempo music fills the hall and two couples among the guests start to dance the jitterbug. After a while, Pat breaks away from the women and steps up on wobbly legs to the top of a coffee table. Holding an imaginary pole, she thrusts her pelvis, wriggles her butt and then performs upper body undulations like a caterpillar, a grin plastered on her face, a glassy look in her eyes. The widened eyes of everyone in the hall stare at her in shock.

Lucas feels heat braising his cheeks and his jaw drops. *Oh shit! She's a former ago-go dancer from Bangkok's red-light district! Dad has lied about her being an ex-cashier.*

Linda's face turns ashen. "Oh, my goodness! This is a disgrace!" She transfers the plate of fruits from her lap to the coffee table. "I better get Dad to take Pat to her room! She's drunk!" She springs to her feet and strides across the hall to the back patio.

The next day...
Seated at the dining table, Oscar takes a gulp of coffee and hears Lucas coming down the staircase. Sitting across him, Pat is buttering a piece of toast. Through the dining room doorway, he sees his son striding across the hallway. "Lucas, you're not eating breakfast?" he asks, his mouth half-filled with cornflakes.

"I'm not sitting at the same table with her!" yells Lucas from the hallway. "I'll be eating out from today onwards." His tone of voice brims with scorn and his usual mug of cocoa, prepared by Pat, is set on the dining table, waiting for him.

Eyebrows inched up in surprise, Oscar gets to his feet. "What do you mean?" He adjusts his trousers with a tug, takes long strides to the hall and stands a few feet away from his son. "I thought you like Pat's Thai dishes."

Togged up in jeans, his face in a scowl, Lucas stops at the door, his hand on the knob, and turns to look over his shoulder. "Not dishes cooked by an ex-bargirl."

"Stop it!" Blood pounds in Oscar's temples like a surging tide. "I'll hear none of that as long as you're staying in this house!"

Lucas opens the door and turns to face Oscar. "I'm sorry, Dad." The fire in his eyes blazes through the thick lenses of his spectacles. "In that case, I'll be moving out soon. I'll buy a motorbike and return the Ford Ranger to you."

Six months later...

Dr. Harrison (not his real name) looks into the eyepiece of the keratometer and slowly turns the focusing knob. "Please look in the centre, Lucas." At the other end of the instrument, which resembles a stout telescope, Lucas is resting his chin on a plastic piece, his heart thumping in his rib cage. Several seconds pass. "Okay, now let me check the other eye." The eye doctor begins to examine Lucas's other eye. "Please remain still...Hmmm...Okay, done." Dr. Harrison sits up straight and Lucas moves his head away from the instrument.

The eye doctor's expression is grim. "I'm afraid your keratoconus has taken a sudden turn for the worse. These soft contact lenses you're wearing now won't do you any good very soon. You need a cornea transplant." He pauses for emphasis. "Otherwise you'll go blind in both eyes." He releases an exhale of apparent frustration. "Donors of corneas are in short supply. So, we'll have to put you on the waiting list – it's quite long, I'm afraid."

Lucas' palms start to sweat and he wipes them against his pants.

A week later...

In his office, Lucas hears the beep of his mobile phone lying in front of him on his desk. He looks away from the computer screen and answers the call. "Hello?" The caller I.D. shows Dr. Harrison's clinic.

"Lucas, I'm Paula, Dr. Harrison's nurse. We've good news for you. There's a cornea ready for your transplant."

"Huh?" Prickles of excitement alert Lucas's senses. "So quickly?"

"The Lord Almighty works in strange ways, Lucas. Praise to the Good Lord!" Paula's tone of voice turns from preachy to serious. "Now, the transplant is an out-patient procedure. It will take about two hours but you'll need someone to drive you home. So, when can you come in?"

Two days later...

Dr. Harrison rounds his desk and plunks down in his swivel chair. "The procedure went smoothly," he says to Lucas. "Sleep with your eye shield on. I'll give you some eye drops and pain medication." He casts his gaze down on a card and writes on it. "After three days, you can remove the eye shield but be careful not to rub your eyes, especially in the middle of your sleep."

Seated across the eye doctor's desk, Lucas nods, his heart swelling with happiness. "I'm curious, doctor. Did someone die in an accident? I mean, from whom did this cornea come from? Initially, you told me the waiting list is long. Then out of the blue, this cornea appeared like manna from heaven."

"No one died in any accident, Lucas." Dr. Harrison removes his spectacles and massages his temples with his thumb and forefinger. "It came from a live donor." He puts his spectacles on his desk and leans back in his chair.

"I see, but who's this person? Can you please tell me?"

The eye doctor sits up straight and puts on his spectacles. "Your stepmother, Mrs. Patcharapa Martin."

Lucas' jaw drops. "Sweet angels of heaven! Oh, my God!" A twinge cramps in his chest.

Linda pushes the door open to the kitchen and enters. Pat is standing at the sink, rinsing vegetables under a running tap, her back facing her. "Pat, my brother wants to say something to you."

Pat turns around, an apron wrapped over her dress, an eye-patch strapped over her left eye.

Limbs feeling like boulders, Lucas enters the kitchen and sinks to his knees. "Pat, please forgive me for way I treated you. I'm so sorry... I've misjudged you." A whimpering sob chocks from his throat. "You're so kind....But why?"

"You're a bookkeeper – you need eyesight. I'm a housewife – one eye is good enough for me." Pat holds Lucas' wrists and pulls him to his feet. "Please move back to stay with us. Let's start afresh as a happy family."

"So, that's the story of my former ago-go dancer." Mamasan Agun lifts a hammer above her head and strikes a nail sticking upright in a sawn-off tree stump. *Thud!* The nail buries itself to its head. "Your turn!" She passes me the hammer.

I clobber a selected nail, amongst several, to the best of my ability. Its shank bends!

"You lose! One more lady's drink for me!" A smile twitches across Mamasan Agun's scarlet lips. "Come, I'll show you some picture postcards Patcharapa sent me from Australia. They're in my office drawer."

* * *

Three years earlier...

Sitting at the writing desk in his hotel room in Silom Road, Luuk van Ark (not his real name), a forty-five-year-old Dutch widower, hears the rumble of thunder outside. He tosses the tourist brochure he's reading on the writing desk, rises and steps to the window. He pulls the curtains apart with both hands. Blurry images of neon lights and luminous shafts of headlights from vehicles stuck in traffic hit him in the face. *Sheesh! A downpour... I'll skip Nana Plaza tonight but call for a social escort instead.* He returns to the writing desk, picks up a room service menu and flips it open. He lifts up the phone and dials room service. "Hello? Room 123 here. I want a Singha beer and *tom kha kai* with rice." He pauses. "How soon will the food arrive? Great."

He drops the receiver back in the telephone cradle, picks up his smart phone from the writing desk and performs an Internet search for social escort agencies. He accesses one site and scans the images of the escorts. A photo of "Vanida" and her bio which says "Newcomer! Thai, 26 years old, 160 cm, 35-23-35, English-speaking, high GFE!" attracts his attention. He calls the agency and books Vanida for twenty-four hours, scheduling the appointment in an hour's time which gives him time to finish his dinner.

One-and-a-half hours later, the door bell rings and Luuk takes long strides to open it. Standing in the doorway is Vanida as she looks in her photo, wearing an off-shoulder floral midi dress and wedges. She has a straight nose, big twinkling eyes and her hair hangs straight down to her shoulders. "Sorry I'm late, traffic's terrible," she says, her sweet curved mouth opening like a rose blooming in fast motion.

Wow! She's gorgeous! "Come on in." Hot blood rushing to his groin, Luuk dips his hands into his trouser pocket and pulls out an envelope. "Here's your payment." He hands over the envelope which he found in a drawer of the writing desk. "Please count the money."

"Payment in an envelope? That's so gentlemanly of you." As Vanida takes the envelope, pulls out some money and starts to count them, Luuk moves to the mini fridge. "Any drink for you? There're soft drinks, beer, rum and fruit juices in packets".

"Coca-Cola." Vanida puts the envelope inside her handbag, takes out her mobile and dials a number. "Everything's okay," she half-whispers. "The client has paid." With a sway of hips, she goes to sit on the edge of the bed, returns her phone to her handbag and places it at her side.

Luuk hands her a can and she pops the tab causing a slight fizz and takes a quick sip. He sits beside her with a glass of beer in one hand.

She crosses her legs at the knees. "What're your plans tonight?" Her hand flies to her mouth. "Uuugh!"

"Are you alright?"

Vanida releases an exhale. "Yes, I'm fine. Slight stomach upset."

"To answer your question, tomorrow you take me sightseeing, but tonight, we just make boom-boom, later if the rains stops, we'll go dancing." Luuk takes a glug of his beer and chats with Vanida about the city's weather and best bars.

The breaking-the-ice session is over in ten minutes and Luuk places a hand on her lap. "Come, let's shower together," he says, fire licking at his groin.

In the bathroom, Luuk and Vanida stand facing each other. She rubs liquid soap on his hairy chest, aims the shower rose ejaculating a spray of water at it and lather forms. Putting the shower rose in its wall-mounted holder, Vanida moves forward and starts to rub her breasts against Luuk's chest in circles. *Great balls of fire! They're boobs of the year! And natural too!* He bends his head down to kiss her lips, and she sticks her tongue inside his mouth, resting her hands on his shoulders. As he deepens the kiss, Luuk holds her face with both hands and runs them through her black satiny hair.

"Don't touch my hair!" Vanida reaches for his wrists and pulls his hands away. "Eeeeeeek!" Her eyebrows furrow, her eyes widen in anger. Her wig comes off! It drops to the wet floor.

Vanida's scalp is dotted with several bald patches each the size of a ten-baht coin while the rest of the area is covered with fine strands of hair. "My wig! Now it's wet!" She sidesteps Luuk, grabs her bathing towel from the hook at the back of the door and wraps it around her upper torso.

"My God!" Luuk's jaw drops. "What happened to you?"

Vanida stoops to pick up her wig, the corners of her mouth turned down. "I-I'm undergoing chemotherapy for cancer." Holding the wig in one hand, Vanida pulls the door open. "Is there a hair dryer here?"

"Yes, it's in the dresser drawer. I'm so sorry." Luuk takes the shower rose from its holder and sprays water on his body to wash the lather off.

Luuk steps into his boxers. "You're sick and shouldn't be escorting."

"I need the money." Vanida holds a hair dryer to blow hot air at her wig resting on top of the dresser. "My father suffered a stroke last year, one side of his body is paralyzed, he can't work anymore."

Luuk starts to put on his pants. "What type of cancer do you have?"

Vanida combs her slender fingers through the wig. "Liver."

"After you're done, let's go to Central Mall." Luuk picks up his long-sleeved shirt lying on the bed and shoves one hand into an armhole. "I want to browse around." He slips the other hand into the second armhole and buttons the shirt.

Vanida tosses her gaze at the reflection of Luuk in the dresser mirror. "You don't want boom-boom?" In the mirror, a man with a slight paunch is tucking the tail of his shirt into his pants. His wide jowly face has a round snub nose and small eyes.

"Maybe later tonight if I'm in the mood." Luud steps behind Vanida, checks his hair in his reflection and ploughs one hand through it.

The next evening, a taxi cruises into the driveway of Luuk's hotel and stops at its entrance with Luuk and Vanida sitting behind. Luuk pays the driver and clambers out with Vanida following behind. The duo approaches the glass doors which slide open and they enter the lobby.

Vanida stops walking when Luuk and she reach the centre of the lobby. "My escort service ends now," she says, turning to face Luuk.

"Thank you for a lovely time."

"Tell me, Luuk, why didn't you have sex with me?"

"Your health's already screwed up, screwing you will screw up my conscience."

Eyes soft with tenderness, she reaches out a gentle palm to touch the side of his face. "You're a good man."

Luuk fishes out his mobile phone from his trouser pocket. "Can I have your phone number?"

"Why?"

"I'd like to know your medical progress."

"Sorry, I don't want to get involved in any relationship until I'm cancer-free. It'll only complicate life for me."

"Be optimistic, please. Everything is temporary. Everything begins and ends and something new begins again. We can just be normal friends, can't we? Come on, your number, please?"

Vanida clucks her tongue, locks gazes with Luuk and remains silent for a moment. Then she gives him the number and he inputs it into his phone's address book.

Luuk flicks his gaze away from the screen of his phone to Vanida. "What's your real name?"

"Ratana Anuwat (a pseudonym)."

"Thanks." Luuk puts his phone back in his trouser side pocket. "My full name's Luuk van Ark."

Two months later...

Loud thumps sound on the front door of Luuk's apartment and he steps out from the kitchen where he was rustling up a Club sandwich. He crosses the living room and opens the door. Two uniformed men are standing outside – one is stocky, the other skinny.

"We're from Immigration," says the stocky man, holding up

a badge in one hand. "Are you Luuk van Ark?"

Hell, what's going on? "Yes, I am."

"You've broken immigration laws by doing business illegally."

"What business?"

"You've a website selling Thai souvenirs. Open the door, please. We're putting you in the detention centre until you're charged in court."

Shit! Heart hammering in his rib cage, Luuk takes the key hanging from a hook on the wall near the wrought-iron door, slips it inside the lock and opens it. *Who can I call for help?* The two men clomp inside in their black shiny boots, and Luuk asks the stocky man, "Can I make a phone call, please?"

The stocky man stands in the doorway foyer and folds his arms over his chest. "Sure." His partner pulls out a handcuff from his belt and holds it in his hand.

Taking several steps away, Luuk fishes out his mobile from his side trouser pocket and calls Ratana's number. She does not answer and the call ends. He dials again. *Answer! Answer, please!* Again there is no answer. *Oh my God! One last attempt!* He re-dials. He hears her voice say "Hello" and a noisy exhale of relief blasts from his lips.

"Ratana, I'm Luuk. I'm back in Bangkok. I'm also in trouble. Some immigration people are in my flat now. Can you help me, please?" He pauses for a moment. "Operating a business illegally, it seems." He casts his gaze at the two men, now standing with arms akimbo. "Hmmm...Okay, you talk to them, please." He moves to the stocky man and thrusts his mobile to him. "My friend wants to talk to you."

Holding the phone to his ear, the stocky man jabbers in Thai language for a while before he returns it to Luuk. "Your girlfriend's coming here. Can you text her this address?" He turns his head to eyeball the furniture in the living room. "Can we sit down to wait for her?"

"Sure." Fiddling with his phone, Luuk sends a text message to Ratana

Half an hour later, Ratana arrives in Luuk's apartment. She sits beside Luuk on the settee to talk with the two men in Thai language for a while. Then they rise and, without uttering a word to Luuk, move to the door to leave. Luuk locks the doors after them and hurries to park himself on a chair across Ratana. "Phew! You saved me!" His face glows with happiness.

Ratana sits up straight, her top straining against her full breasts. "Tomorrow, you've to take down your website. Otherwise, they'll come again, understand?"

"Sure." Luuk cocks his head. "You want a drink?"

Ratana gives a gentle wave of her hand. "When did you come back?"

"Two weeks ago. I was busy sourcing for products to sell. I had wanted to call you later and then this thing happened. Months ago, back in Utrecht, I sent you a few text messages but you didn't reply."

"A long-distance friendship is troublesome."

"How's your health?"

"I'm in partial remission." A ghost of a smile hovers on Ratana's lips. "I'm no longer an escort. My brother has found a job in Korat. So my burden has lessened." She shifts in her seat and adjusts her form-fitting skirt. "I'm now a supervisor in a supermarket."

"That's good news and I'm happy for you." Luuk's lips ease into a grin. "I'll be migrating here soon." He blinks, eyes appearing eager to reveal his plans. "When I get a Thai business partner, I'll sell my house in Utrecht and make Pattaya my new home." He glances at his wrist watch. "Can we go out for dinner?"

Ratana's eyes seem to sparkle. "Sure." She hitches her handbag higher up her shoulder and rises from the settee.

Another two months pass...

Seated at his office desk, Luuk lifts the handset of the telephone at his side off its cradle and dials Ratana's number. "Hello there, Ratana, about the part-time maid, did you find anyone?"

"Yes, she's coming over this evening at 7 p.m. I hope you find her suitable."

"Great. Bye."

Back in Bangkok for the third time, Luuk is now co-owner of a travel and tour agency with a Thai partner. During his sojourn in Utrecht, he and Ratana have been in touch by emails and phone text messages.

Inside his apartment, at 7 p.m., Luuk hears the doorbell ring and he goes to open the teak door. Ratana is standing outside, wearing a smile on her face and a sunny floral print dress. Luuk unlocks the wrought-iron door. "Where's the maid?"

"You're looking at her."

"Gee! You're full of surprises!" Luud's gentle chuckle brings a quirk to Ratana's lips. "Come on in."

Ratana steps inside and kicks off her flats.

Luuk closes the wrought-iron door and locks it. "Are you serious?" He slams the teak door shut.

Ratana turns to look at Luuk. "Of course. I can come on Monday, Wednesday and Friday in the morning before I do my afternoon shift."

Luuk puts a hand to the small of her back to guide her to the kitchen. "Come, let me show you where the mop, steam iron and vacuum cleaner are kept."

Two months later...

Ratana finishes vacuuming the living room and goes to the kitchen with a basket of clothes. From a cabinet drawer in the kitchen, she takes out a steam iron. Then she opens the door of a small wall closet, flips down the ironing board and begins to iron the clothes. Soon, she takes a pile of ironed clothes to Luuk's bedroom and places them on his bed. She opens the doors of his clothes wardrobe to hang his shirts. Her eyes span wider in surprise. On a low shelf is a deflated silicon female doll with hair on its head.

What's this? Ratana picks up the doll, holds it by its neck and it unfurls to its full length. *Oh Lord Buddha! It's a sex doll!* A thingamabob which resembles a torch light on one end of the same shelf grabs her attention. *Now, what's this gadget?* Returning the sex doll to its former place, she picks up the widget and pushes a switch. The gizmo releases a whirring sound and vibrates. *Oh my goodness, this is a motorized masturbator! Never knew Luuk has a dark side! No, I can't carry on this relationship with a sex pervert!* She switches off the sex toy and returns it to the shelf. *I can't imagine how our sex life will be like if we end up together.*

An hour later, Ratana locks both doors of the apartment. She gets down on one knee outside the wrought-iron door and slips a ring of two keys under its bottom gap. With a flick of her middle finger, she sends the keys – given by Luuk to her – sliding into the doorway foyer. As she starts to walk down the corridor, she sends a text message to Luuk: *I accidentally discovered your sex toys. Very disappointed and upset. Your keys on the floor in your flat.*

Let's split. Have fun with your sex toys.

In the lift foyer, Ratana jabs the button "G" on the side panel and waits. Her phone rings and the caller ID shows it's Luuk. She ignores the call.

Two days later...

At closing time, the security guard pulls one of two shutters of the entrance in Hot-Mart down and locks it. He yanks the other shutter halfway down and the supermarket's staff leaves by ducking it. As Ratana traipses out of the supermarket, Luuk approaches her, stopping a few feet away.

Ratana stops dead in her tracks. "Didn't I tell you we're through?" Her eyes narrow in annoyance. "There's no scarcity of girls in Patpong and you still play with sex toys huh?" She scrunches her face in disgust. "You're a pervert whom I don't want to get involved with." She begins to walk away briskly, her heels clicking on the marble floor.

Luuk takes long strides after her. "Ratana, please let me explain." He matches her stride. "Those sex toys are not mine. I got them for my son. He's coming to Pattaya soon for a long vacation."

"Oh my goodness!" Ratana turns her head to glare at Luuk. "Father and son sharing sex toys! Two perverts in the family!"

"That's not what I meant." Luuk scratches his head and checks his watch. "Come to my apartment, please. There's only one way to convince you. I want you to talk with my son's doctor over the webcam. It's afternoon in Holland now so his clinic is still open." He fishes out his mobile phone. "I'll call him to get ready for the webcam call. Please give me a fair chance to explain, okay?"

"Alright, then." Ratana casts him a skewed glance.

Inside his apartment, Luuk clicks on the webcam icon on his laptop, with Ratana sitting at his side on the settee. An image of a half-bald man wearing a necktie appears on the screen.

"Good afternoon, Dr. Willemsen (a pseudonym). Sorry for this inconvenience."

"No bother at all, Luuk."

"Dr. Willemsen, can you please explain my son's condition to my girlfriend Ratana?"

The good doctor clears his throat. "Ahem...Bram, Luuk's son, is a sex addict. He was in prison for a short time for indecent behavior – masturbating in a public place to be exact. After his release, he has been undergoing therapy with me voluntarily. Apart from giving him counseling, I've prescribed medications. I also recommended those sex toys in case he can't control his sexual urges. Those sex toys have nothing to do with Mr. Luud van Ark who is a fine gentleman."

"Thank you, doctor." Turing to Ratana, Luuk says, "My son can't bring the sex toys in from Holland so I got them from a street vendor in Patpong for him."

Back to the present...
Mummy Ratana picks up the handset from the telephone on her desk and jabs the intercom button. "Bram, can you come here for a moment, please?" She drops the handset back to the telephone cradle.

I and Mummy Ratana, owner of Silky Soapy Massage (not its real name) in Huai Khwang district, are shoehorned inside her cubicle office. The massage parlour offers erotic lingam massage, body-to-body massage, fetish silk stocking massage and soapy massage with happy ending.

Moments later, the door of the cubicle opens and a short stout man –probably in his early twenties – garbed in blue jeans and a t-shirt enters. He has pointy ears and a round snub nose.

"Bram, this is Joseph, he's a writer from Kuala Lumpur." Ratana tosses her gaze at me. "Please say hello to him."

I nod at Bram. "How do you do?"

"G-G-Good, p-pleased t-to m-meet y-you, s-sir." Bram looks from me to his step-mother. "R-R-Ratana, the l-laundrette p-phoned. T-They s-said t-they c-can't send the towels t-today b-because t-two of their m-m-machines broke down. And just n-now, a c-c-customer who s-s-screwed Na-Nattaporn c-complained of l-l-lousy service b-b-by her."

"Thanks, I'll have a word with her afterward."

Bram goes away.

Mummy Ratana leans back in her chair. "Bram is very shy with girls because of his bad stutter but...." She gives a gentle shake of her head. "Dr. Willemsen didn't cure him of his sex addiction and he had difficulty getting a job in Holland. So after Luuk married me, he brought Bram to work here so that his son can have all the sex he wants."

My eyebrows shoot upward. "What!"

"But the three of us are a happy family."

8

Saigon:
Jaunt on a Scooter

The glass door of the hotel lobby swings inward and a late-twenties girl wearing a helmet and beige *ao dai* over dark pants ambles in. She is plump and another helmet dangles by its strap from her left hand. Her pasty face has a squashed nose between rosy cheeks and her vivacious brown eyes sparkle with intelligence.

I rise from my seat and walk up to her. "Are you from the scooter tour company?"

"Yes. My name's Thanh." She extends her pudgy right hand. "You booked the customized nightlife tour, isn't it?"

"Yes, the naughty places." I pump her plump hand. "My name's Jackson." Her hand feels like a big slab of brown tofu.

"Please put on your helmet." As I strap the helmet on, she says, "We'll go to Backpacker Street, Butterfly Park, Little Japan, Gay Street and Blowjob Street. You can stop at any nightspot and go in for a look but I cannot accompany you inside, understand? That's our company's policy."

She leads me to her scooter parked at the kerb and we climb aboard.

"Okay, here we go!" She engages the gear with a loud *cluck!*

The front wheel of the scooter leaps up like a rearing stallion!

"Eeewwww!" My heart rises in my throat and beats like a bongo drum.

"Sorry, I'm new on the job!" Thanh giggles. "I just joined last week, I'm not used to this scooter."

Sucking in a calming breath, she gently twists the throttle and we join the stream of traffic. After a few left and right turns, the neon sign Crazy Buffalo looms before me as we enter Bui Vien Street and exhaust fumes almost choke me.

"This road is closed to traffic on Saturday and Sunday nights from 7 p.m. to 2 a.m."

I observe the foot traffic rather than the neon signs blinking yellow, purple and red at me. "I don't see many street working ladies."

"It's still early. Come around midnight. You'll find many working ladies to interview easily. No need to be scared. This is a tourist area. There're many security cameras around."

Almost at the end of the drag, we turn into a side road and make a loop to Pham Ngu Lao Street, also known as Backpacker Street. The scene reminds me of Khao San Road in Bangkok as it is filled with restaurants, massage shops, nightclubs, beer bars and cafes. As we pass Vien Dong Hotel, Thanh says, "Vien Dong Spa is inside that hotel. Opens twenty-hours. This is Saigon's most famous spa because it has pretty girls. You can have either a standard room or VIP room with jacuzzi."

"Got gay spa?"

"Of course. Later, I'll show you gay spas." She looks straight for a second and turns her head sideways to say, "Now we go to Butterfly Park, always have night butterflies, or ladies of the night." Looking ahead at the drag again, she revs the engine to pick up speed and soon we are cruising past a dimly lit park, with dark silhouettes of trees and people walking. "This is 23rd September Park. Sometimes shortened to 23/9 Park. Sit here during the evening and night butterflies will come to offer you sex."

At the next junction, Thanh makes a loop and we head northwest to District 10. After a fifteen-minute ride, we end up in Hoa Hung Street where Thanh points out Guy Spa and Nam Spa, which are for men only.

"All massage boys are eighteen to twenty-five only," says Thanh, stopping in front of Nam Spa, housed in a French-style colonial house, surrounded by a perimeter stone wall. "They're handsome and muscular."

"How you know?"

"You can check their Facebook accounts. Why don't you go in for a look?"

I get off the scooter, enter the gate entrance and find myself in a calm-inducing garden profuse with foliage. I step inside the building, walk up to a counter and am greeted by a young, friendly receptionist. He shows me an iPad with photos of their "technicians" – that's what their masseurs are referred to – and a list of services available. Then I return to the scooter. "Yes, it's a beautiful place," I say to Thanh. "Lots of greenery and water features that create a relaxing ambience."

From here, we head back to District 1 and, partway, make a detour to pass a four-star hotel. "This luxury hotel has a posh spa with a two-price structure," says Thanh, pointing at the building bathed in orange-hued lights. "Inclusive of tip or without tip. Choose the cheaper price and they'll send a woman who's somebody's grandmother to massage you. A few other hotel-spas also have this price gimmick."

Now, we enter Le Thanh Ton Street, known as Little Japan. By comparison to Pham Ngu Lao Street and Bui Vien Street, this enclave is less chaotic. Noodle houses, shabu shabu restaurants, massage parlours, karaoke bars and hostess bars pass by me as Thanh follows the flow of the traffic without slowing down. "Tokyo Spa is popular here," she says, "because of its beautiful massage ladies." Then Thanh swerves into a side alley. The small joints here look seedier, with girls hanging outside, some sitting atop their parked scooters.

From Little Japan, a ten-minute ride takes us to De Tham Street aka Gay Street, according to Thanh. She eases the throttle and we cruise down the drag like a legless cockroach. "Tipsy Unicorn, Republic Lounge, Whisky & Wares and THI Bar are located around this area. They're all gay-friendly. There's another exciting spot called Full Disclosure, and it's in Ly Tu Trong. They've monthly LGBT parties." Further down, Thanh points to a woman sitting at the sidewalk near a budget hotel with a small display rack filled with packets of cigarettes. "Ah! There she is!" She stops the scooter at the side of the road and rests both feet on the ground. "You want to buy happy-weed cigarette?"

"What's that?"

"Marijuana cigarette."

"Sure – just one will do."

We get off the scooter and Thanh parks it on the kerb. We tramp up to the fortyish woman and Thanh says something to her in Vietnamese language. The woman picks out a particular cigarette box. She looks around as if to make sure no cops are nearby, then takes out a rolled cigarette from the box and hands it to Thanh who passes it to me. "Thirty thousand," Thanh says.

I pay the cigarette vendor and ask Thanh, "Do lots of Vietnamese smoke marijuana?"

"This woman moves around, sometimes she's here, sometimes

she's in Bui Vien and Pham Ngu Lao. So most of her customers are tourists."

I hold the cigarette to my nose, take a deep sniff and a sweetish fragrance teases my olfactory senses. As we walk back to the scooter, I tear away the paper, pour the happy weed on one palm and take another sniff which jolts me. I scatter the happy weed away before I climb on Thanh's scooter.

From De Tham Street, we zip alongside the bank of the Saigon River for a short distance and then head northwest to Nguyen Phi Khanh Street on the fringe of District 1, and, according to Thanh, the drag has earned the nickname Blowjob Street.

Thanh stops the scooter at the kerb of the street which is filled with rather drab buildings on both sides. "Our locals called it *Hot Toc* Street. *Hot Toc* means cutting hair," says Thanh.

I cast my gaze far and wide. Tucked amongst shuttered stores and open stores are several men's barber shops. "Please wait here – I wanna check them out." I get off the scooter and enter the nearest one which has a revolving red-and-white pole.

Inside the hall, several girls in spaghetti-strap tops and miniskirts are lounging on a settee at one side. The rest of the place is taken up with barber chairs and a small cashier's counter. An older woman, obviously the mamasan, rises from the barber's chair she is sitting on and walks up to me.

"Welcome!" Her mascared eyes crinkle with a warm smile.

"I want a haircut." With two fingers I make a scissor-like cutting motion.

"All lady barbers gone out, no haircut." The mamasan waves her hand to stress her answer. "You want massage with blowjob happy ending?"

Her audacity almost snatches my breath away. "Huh? Oh,

never mind, thank you."

I exit the shop and step up to a second *hot toc* salon about forty feet down the road. The door swings inward before I can push it and I enter. Inside, the setup is again like a typical barber's shop, and there are a few girls sitting in a small lounge at one corner.

A sex kitten, possibly in her twenties, who pulled the door closes it and I say to her, "I want a shave and a haircut."

"Sorry, no barber, all barbers on leave today." The sex kitten's red lips upturn in a sweet smile. "But we've special services. You want?" She takes a step forward into my private space, her perfume wafting to my nostrils. "You can choose your girl."

I feign a half-smile. "No, thank you." I open the door, leave and walk to my waiting scooter.

Soon, Thanh drops me at the entrance of my hotel. As I climb down from her scooter and return her helmet, she says, "Thank you for taking this tour. There's another naughty thing I couldn't show you because it's found on the Internet. Type in '*gai goi* Saigon' on Google and you'll get websites offering call girls who'll come to your hotel, if your hotel is girl-friendly. Just translate the Vietnamese text in the websites to English."

Later, as I lie in bed inside my room, I ponder on the possibility of interviewing a *gai goi* for my next book *Saigon Undercover*.

* * *

George Ma (not his real name), a thirtyish tourist from Bedok, Singapore, steps out of the en-suite bathroom stark naked and moves to the clothes closet. "Dear, I'm going out for a couple of beers," he says to his wife, taking out a t-shirt from a hook.

"Coming along?" He slips the t-shirt over his head, picks out a pair of boxers and puts them on.

"I'm pooped, I need a nap," says Mrs. Ma, lying on the bed. "Take the room key with you. Wake me up when you're back, maybe we can go for supper."

George starts to wear his khaki shorts. "Sure, we'll try that Vietnamese restaurant in Pasteur Street we saw yesterday. Err... what's its name? Never mind, we can find it easily." He moves to the door, slips on his sneakers and leaves.

Sitting in the sidewalk of a beer bar in Pham Ngu Lao Street, George is guzzling Saigon Green from a bottle when a motorcyclist stops at the side of the road in front of him. She gets off her old Yamaha motorbike, takes off her helmet and runs her fingers through her shoulder-length hair.

Smiling, she steps up to George's table. "Hello, darling, you want boom-boom?" She is petite and has a small nose and rosebud-shaped kissable lips.

A flood of heat rushes to George's loins as he latches his gaze at her décolletage in her skimpy top. "Price?"

"Two million dong, one-hour service." Uninvited, she pulls out a chair and sits across George.

"No, one million, five hundred."

"No discount. I give high GFE. We can cuddle, kiss and talk until your time is up."

George flicks his gaze at the traffic and back to the floozie. "Okay, can we use a short-time love motel? My friend's in my hotel room."

"We can use my flat, two hundred thousand extra."

"How far away?"

"Ten minutes only, near Nguyen Cu Trinh Street."

"But you send me back to my hotel – Viumung Inn."

"No problem." The girl rises and smiles. "I'm Quyen."

The next morning...

Inside his hotel room, George steps out of the bathroom stark naked and a minty exhale rolls from his lips. "Your turn, dear." Facing glowing with happiness, he recalls yesterday's high-GFE session with Quyen which stretched to two hours and included a cat nap in her arms. As he dries his hair with a bath towel, he starts to hum a lively song.

Her gaze raking her husband from head to toe, Mrs. Ma gets to a sitting position in bed. "In the name of hell, where did you go last night?"

"Huh? I want for a couple of drinks, walked around a bit."

The flicker of a temper glints in Mrs. Ma's eyes. "You're lying!"

George tosses the towel on the dresser chair. "Come on, dear, please don't spoil our vacation with your jealousy tantrums." His tone of voice is casual.

"Look at yourself in the mirror! Which hooker's bed did you lie down on? How did you get bitten by bed bugs?"

George steps in front of the dresser mirror. His jaw drops! His body is covered with red welts.

9

Saigon:
Nocturnal Viet Cong Dolls

The clothing stores, moneychangers and travel agencies have closed along the drag, leaving the neon lights of bars, spas and nightclubs to lure customers. Clusters of motorbikes are parked intermittently along the sidewalk and every nightspot I pass is blasting techno music from its doorway.

About thirty feet after I've passed a twenty-hour convenience store, a slender long-haired woman takes two steps forward on stilettos from her spot on the sidewalk and blocks my way. Garbed in a black bare-back top, she is tall, almost flat-chested but has shapely legs protruding from beneath a red mini skirt.

"Want massage with happy ending?" she asks, her lips upturned in a smile. "It's late, so I give you discounted price! Five hundred thousand dong" She looks like she's in her mid-twenties and has a long face but a round chin.

I stop in my tracks and catch a whiff of sweat intermingled with perfume. "No, thank you." I flash a wry smile, sidestep her and continue to walk ahead.

The woman turns on her heels and walks in stride beside me. "How much can you pay?"

"I'm not interested."

"You gay?"

I do not reply and she points ahead to a man sitting astride the back carrier of a stationary bicycle with both feet resting on the ground. "That's my husband – he's a massage boy. He can give massage with full service."

We stop a few feet away from the massage boy, probably in his late-twenties, and the girl says something to him in Vietnamese language and he replies in the same language. The woman returns her attention to me but before she can speak, I ask, "He's your legal husband?"

"Of course!" Her cherry-red thin lips curl upward. "We've marriage certificates."

Sweet Jesus! What an interesting pair! I toss my gaze at the massage boy, who has a square face and a block chin. "Can you tell me how you met your wife and married her? I'll pay the price of a massage for your time." He is wearing a t-shirt with the Quiksilver logo on its centre and a pair of dark flared pants.

The big eyes of the massage boy gleam with apparent excitement. "Are you serious?" His English is strongly accented.

"Of course." I pull out my wallet. "I can pay half now, half later."

The massage boy gets off the back carrier, props his bicycle on its side stand and stands next to it. "My wife's English is better than mine," he says, thrusting his chin at the floozie. "It's better that she talks with you." He dips his hands in his trouser pockets

"I'm Tuyet," says the girl, sticking out her hand. "Let's shake hand on a deal. No need to make part payment."

I pump her hand firmly and it rewards me with a spongy feel. "I'm Jimmy from Singapore," I lie.

The moment I release Tuyet's hand, the massage boy reaches for my hand. "Thank you, Jimmy. My name's Quang."

I take his hand for a second, then drop it like dog poop as it is sticky with sweat. I return my attention to Tuyet. "Can we find a place to sit?"

Tuyet and Quang exchange some remarks in Vietnamese language and the former says to me, "Let's go to a late-night restaurant nearby." She starts to walk and points to the street ahead. "Second left down the road."

Ten minutes later, we are sitting in a fan-ventilated restaurant with plastic tables and chairs. About half of the tables are taken up by patrons and a fat waitress garbed in a frumpy dress comes to our table.

I rest my elbows on the table. "I just want some snacks and a drink," I say, studying her face in the bright light.

"The soup here is delicious." Tuyet places her handbag on her lap and tosses her hair back. "And some spring rolls?" She crosses her legs at the knees, tugs the hem of her mini skirt down and leans back in her chair.

"Sure, and lime soda for me."

Tuyet casts a side gaze at the waitress, places an order in Vietnamese language and looks at me. "Where do you want me to start?"

"Tell me something about your husband first."

Two years ago...

Sitting in the mail room, twenty-five-year-old Quang, a despatch rider for a trading company in the Central Business District, is sorting out the letters and packages in his out-tray and mentally planning his route for the day. His handphone on his desk buzzes and the caller I.D. shows his father. Quang ignores it. As the phone continues to buzz, he recalls an incident several years ago...

In his bedroom, sixteen-year-old Quang looks at himself in

the full-length mirror of his clothes wardrobe. He has wanted to kiss a boy for some time but has been unable to find a partner. Locking gazes with the eyes in the mirror, he leans forward and kisses his own reflection, his tongue licking its shiny surface.

"Quang!" His father's voice booms from the doorway. "What're you doing?" The tone of his voice is like a tiger's growl.

Dammit! He forgot to close the door!

"Bloody hell, you're learning to become a gay, huh?" His brawny father, a construction labourer, steps into the room and unbuckles his belt. "And where did you learn that?" He tugs out his belt from the hoops of his pants and holds the two ends together. "I want you to be a normal boy, you understand? Now, you need to be punished so that you can be cured of your perversion!" With a snarl, he whips Quang repeatedly on the shoulders and upper arms with the belt until he cries like a baby.

From that day, Quang has suppressed his sexuality which has become a taboo subject within the family. A year later, he dropped out of school and, from the small town of Ben Cat, he came to Saigon to work. Henceforth, he has seldom communicated with his father.

The buzzing of the handphone stops and Quang picks up the letters in his in-tray meant for distribution to the office staff spread over two floors. As he is scrutinizing the names on the envelopes, his handphone buzzes again. The call is from his younger sister.

Tossing several letters on the table, he reaches for his handphone. "Yes?"

"Brother, why didn't you answer *Cha's* [Papa's] call?"

"Aw...you know I don't like to talk to him, unless it's absolutely necessary."

"Something bad happened. *Me* [Mum] has been diagnosed

with kidney disease. She needs dialysis every week. You need to send more money home."

"Dammit! Where am I going to find the extra money?"

"I'll be completing my studies in two years' time. So, it's impossible to stop now. I'm sure you're resourceful enough to sort out this problem. Bye-bye."

The line goes dead.

Quang expands and contracts his ribcage with a heavy sigh, leans back in his chair and ponders for a while. He sits up straight again and jabs his friend's number on his handphone.

"Hello, Dung, convenient to talk now?"

"Sure, what's up?"

"Any part-time work in your bar? I'm looking for side income."

"Not at the moment. Why don't you call Trung? I heard he's working in a sauna."

"I want flexible hours."

"Why not become a freelance massage boy? Just cycle around the tourist areas to pick up clients."

"I don't have a bicycle."

"I can lend you mine – for a small fee, of course. That's to compensate for the wear and tear on my bicycle tyres."

Quang runs his hand through his thick hair. "Gee, thanks!"

Cool night air feathers his face as Quang cycles slowly and rings his bicycle bell as he passes a man traipsing along the drag bustling with other pedestrians. "Massage, sir?" he asks, stopping his bicycle a few feet ahead.

The portly pedestrian – a foreigner – shakes his head. "Nope."

"Thank you, sir." Quang nods and continues ahead. *Aha! A*

blond balding head. He rings his bicycle bell, overtakes the man and stops in front of him. "Massage, sir?" asks Quang, turning his head to look at the Westerner.

"Full service?" His squeaky voice belies his rugged appearance.

"Of course, sir! Five hundred thousand dong – forty-five minutes." Quang swings one leg off the saddle off his bicycle, holds the handlebars and stands beside the vehicle. "Where's your hotel?"

"Hoa Hong Inn (name changed) – further up on the other side."

After the deed is done, Quang steps out of the hotel and saunters in sneakers to his bicycle parked near a lamp post on the sidewalk. He hitches the strap of a small bag off his shoulder and slips it over the handle bar of his bicycle. As he bends over to open its wheel-lock, two young men step up to him. Quang straightens up and returns their stares.

"You massage boy?" asks the bigger of the two, who has an unshaven chin and Mohican hair-cut.

Quang assesses the big beefy stranger. *Hell, he looks dangerous!* "Yes, why?"

The second man asks, "You serviced a customer just now?" In his early twenties, he is clean-shaven and has on a light-coloured t-shirt and dark track pants.

"What's that to you?"

The clean-shaven man thrusts out his hand, palm facing upward. "Give me the payment!"

Ire heats Quang's cheeks, matching the fire in his eyes. "Why?"

"This is my territory." The clean-shaven man's tone of voice is as hard as the concrete of the sidewalk. "You cannot solicit clients here."

The heat in Quang's cheeks shoots straight to his temper. "Go to hell!"

A fist flies from the clean-shaven man to the side of Quang's face but he parries it away with one arm. In the next fraction of a second, the beefy man unleashes an uppercut to Quang's chin which snaps his head upward. Quang staggers backward several steps, falling flat on his back. As he lays face-up on the pavement in a daze, the beefy man stomps a boot on his chest! *Oh hell! That's a size 22 boot!* Then a kick lands on the side of Quang's head and he passes out.

"What happened? Can you get up?"

A woman's gentle voice pulls Quang back to consciousness and he rubs the side of his head where he was kicked. Slowing regaining his senses, he sees a woman squatting at his side. She is wearing low-waist jeans and a cropped top which exposes a navel ring. The woman helps him to a sitting position.

"Aaugh...my head hurts." Quang releases a noisy exhale. "Two thugs beat me up."

The woman points to a wallet a few feet away from Quang's side. "Is that yours?"

"Yes, it's mine!" Scooting sideways on his butt, Quang stretches forward to pick the wallet and returns to a sitting position. He opens the wallet, peers inside and his jaw drops. "My money's been stolen!"

The woman stands up. "I gotta go – you take care, okay?" She starts to walk away, her shadow becoming smaller on the sidewalk.

Quang gets to his feet but dizziness forces him to squat and, moments later, he crawls to his bicycle, still parked at the lamp post. *Oh shit!* Both the tyres of his bicycle are flat. *They did something to the tyres.*

"Miss! Miss!" Quang hollers, gripping the saddle of the bicycle as he hefts himself to a standing position.

The woman looks over her shoulder, turns and walks back, her hips swaying from side to side. She stops a few feet from Quang and asks, "Yes, what's the problem now?"

"Can you lend me some money? I need to take a taxi back. My bicycle's tyres are flat."

"How I know you'll repay me?"

"Don't you trust me?"

"I only trust myself." Her tone of voice is stoic.

"Please, I've to work tomorrow morning." Quang's eyes plead for understanding. "I need to get home to catch some sleep."

"Why don't you sleep here to guard your bicycle?"

"Is your place nearby? I'll push my bicycle to your place, leave it there. Tomorrow, when I come to repay you, I'll collect it."

"Now you're talking some sense." A shadow of a smile hovers on her cherry-red lips. "Alright."

"My name's Quang." He extends his hand. "What's yours?"

The woman grasps his hand lightly. "I'm Tuyet. Why were you beaten up?"

From the sidewalk, Tuyet heads towards a metal door beside the closed shutters of a launderette, unlocks it and swings it open inward with a squeak. "I stay on the first floor," she says, casting a backward glance at Quang, holding his bicycle by its handlebars.

Tuyet steps inside and flicks on a light switch on one wall. An overhead bulb lights up, illuminating a flight of cement steps and

Tuyet starts to vault up. "Come, bring your bicycle in." She stops at the top landing.

Quang lifts his bicycle up from the ground by its top tube and lumbers up the staircase where Tuyet is waiting on the landing. She opens a wooden door, enters a corridor with Quang following behind, huffing and puffing, his arms straining from the weight of the bicycle.

Tuyet enters the dining room, which is occupied with a table and several stools and switches on the light. "You can put your bicycle here," she says.

Quang puts the bicycle down beside one wall, locks it and hands the key to Tuyet. "Can you lend me fifty thousand?"

"So much?"

"The bicycle's tyres have been slashed. They've to be replaced." Quang takes out his handphone from his side trouser pocket. "Give me your number so I can give you a miss call."

"Sure." Tuyet opens her handbag and drops the bicycle key in. "Six-three-four-five-one-eight-right." She takes out some money notes and hands them over to Quang. Moments later, she hears a short buzz from her mobile inside her hand bag.

Quang moves away from the dining room and Tuyet follows him. "Who else stays here?" He starts to climb down the cement stairs.

"Two other girls, same profession as me."

Quang opens the metal door and turns to face Tuyet. "Goodnight."

"Same to you – take care." Tuyet closes the door and locks it.

Strolling with Trung and Dung, Quang scans the drag ahead and the sidewalks on both sides. People in pairs, lone men and party animals in groups – their faces illuminated by the neon lights of nightspots – are sauntering along the sidewalks, while touts and street hookers are hovering in their spots, looking for customers.

"There! That's him!" Quang points to the clean-shaven massage boy whom he encountered three days ago. "Come, let's go – you two walk abreast and I'll walk behind so he can't see me."

Garbed in shiny black pants, Mr. Clean-shaven is standing across the drag outside a budget hotel. Quang and his two friends cross the drag to approach him. When the trio is a few feet away, Trung and Dung dart forward to Mr. Clean-shaven's sides, each gripping one upper arm. His eyes span wider when Quang steps up to him, stopping an arm's length away.

"Well, well, your big friend isn't here tonight, huh?" Quang shows an open palm and flaps it a few times. "Give me back my money! And compensation for the beating!"

"Alright! Alright! Release my arms first!" He dips his hand inside his side trouser pocket, takes out his wallet and hands some money notes over to Quang who slips them inside his shirt pocket.

The stocky-and-ugly Trung shoves a big hairy fist in the man's face. "This massage boy has joined our gang, understand? He's one of us now." Trung grinds out the words between big clenched teeth. "Tomorrow, he's working this territory again. If you hurt him, we'll come after you." He glances around to make sure no one is watching and pulls out a switchblade handle from his back trouser pocket. "If you want war, we can give you a bloody war." He presses a button and a shiny blade protrudes from the handle. "Understand?"

Fear glazes Mr. Clean-shaven's eyes "I-I guess this territory's big enough for both of us."

HR manager Thao slams a pudgy fist on her desk. "Quang, this is the fourth time you've been late for work this month." She adjusts her cat eye spectacles. "What's your excuse?" Saliva sputters from her mouth as she speaks.

Scrunching his nose, Quang leans back in his chair. *Sheesh! She's got bad breath!* "Err, too many late nights watching TV and playing video games."

Thao opens a folder file in front of her and pulls out two sheets of paper. "This is a warning letter." He places them in front of Quang. "Please sign both copies and give me the duplicate."

Quang pulls out a ballpoint pen from his shirt pocket and scribbles on the dotted line on both copies. He returns the pen to his shirt pocket and hands over one copy to Thao.

"One more warning letter and you're out!" hollers Thao, slipping the letter inside her folder file.

Quang covers his nose with one hand, rises and leaves the room with the letter.

Back in the mail room, Quang dials Tuyet's number. His call is unanswered and he re-dials.

"Hello?" Tuyet's voice sounds sleepy. "What's so urgent that you need to wake me up?"

"Do you know of any room to let around your area? I need to stay nearer to my working territory so that I can go to office on time."

"You're lucky – one of the girls here is moving out end of the month. I'll text you my landlady's phone number. You talk to her yourself. Bye."

"Thanks."

Inside his room, Quang pulls open the door and leaves it ajar.

Grabbing the handlebars of his bicycle, he pushes it out and locks the door. He wheels his bicycle down the corridor and stops outside Tuyet's room. He raps on the door with one hand. "Tuyet! Tuyet!" There is no answer.

Since becoming Tuyet's flat-mate three months ago, Quang and she have been eating dinner daily before working the streets. Occasionally, Suong, the third tenant, joins them but mostly she eats with her boyfriend.

Quang calls Tuyet on his handphone and she answers immediately, "Yes, Quang?"

"Tuyet, where are you?"

"I'm on the rooftop."

"Doing what?"

"Thinking, relaxing, enjoying the views. Come join me."

Quang props his bicycle on its side stand, sprints down the corridor to the front door and opens it. He pounds up the staircase to the fourth floor and steps through the doorway of the rooftop hatch where its door has been left open. A fluorescent light above the doorway and light from an adjacent tower are the only sources of illumination. Standing at the perimeter wall, Tuyet casts her gaze upward to Quang. "Come and look down. The cars and buses below look like toys."

I'd prefer to be in hell than in this place! "I'm afraid of heights." His heart pounds in his chest.

Tuyet walks toward him and stretches an arm. "Come, hold my hand."

Quang grabs her hand and shuffles behind her to the waist-high wall. "I dare not look down," he says, casting his gaze upward at the stars.

Dropping his left hand, she hooks her right arm round his

waist. "Close your eyes and tilt your head downward." Her left hand reaches for his right hand and holds it.

Heat jolts through Quang at her touch, and he squeezes his eyes shut and drops his head. His crotch starts to throb, an experience he's never experienced when he's with a girl.

"Now open your eyes." Tuyet squeezes his right hand. "You're safe with me holding you."

Taking a fortifying breath, Quang does as he is told. "Oh, such a nice view. The people down there are like ants."

"To fight your inner fears, you must confront them, not run away."

They gaze at the scene below in silence for a while.

Quang flips his gaze upward to Tuyet. "I've wanted to say something to you for some time, Tuyet."

Tuyet's eyelashes flip upward. "Yes?"

Quang hesitates for a moment. "I love you, Tuyet."

"What!" Tuyet's lips quirk in a grin. "But you're not straight, you're bent! So how can you love a woman?"

Quang's face sags from gladsome to hurt. "Truth is I've been having this attraction for you since the day you helped me out. At first, it felt strange to me but now, I'm sure my feeling for you is love."

"You should go to church to pray your gay away first!" A chuckle breezes from Tuyet's lips. "Then only you can talk about loving a woman." She drops her hands at her sides to release him and starts to walk away. "Come, let's get a bite." Her voice is filled with mirth.

Her words lance Quang's heart and he squares his shoulders to shake off the hurt.

Bob-haired Suong cuts a piece of her *banh heo* with a spoon. "Where's your lover boy?" She spoons the blob of water-fern cake into her open mouth and starts to chew.

"Went to a watch store to have his watch repaired." Tuyet lifts a piece of *banh khot* and chomps on it. "He's not my lover boy."

Suong and Tuyet are eating dinner in a hawker stall in an alley off Nguyen Trai Street, District 1, only ten minutes' walk from their flat.

"But I noticed that he makes breakfast for you before going for work and leaves it on the kitchen island with a note." Suong lifts a glass to her cupid-bow lips and sips a splash of *nuoc sam*.

Tuyet shoves the remainder of the *banh khot* into her mouth. "He's a soulmate, a good friend and a gay." He digs out a piece of tissue paper from her handbag and wipes her fingers.

"He's probably bi and is in love with you." Suong blinks her small eyes. "And a gay can become straight."

A month later...
Quang knocks on the door of Suong's room and she opens it halfway. She is dressed in a spaghetti strap top and a mini skirt. "Yes?" The smell of frangipani wafts from her perfume.

"Suong, where's Tuyet? I called her mobile a few times but it's switched off."

"Gone back to her home village. She left by bus this morning. Earlier, her brother called to inform her that her husband and father were killed in a motorcycle accident."

"What!" Quang's lips part in shock. "She never told me she's married! Where's her village? She needs me."

"In the outskirt of Binh Ngoc, but there's no bus going there at night. You'll have to wait until tomorrow morning."

"I'll leave tonight by motorbike." He checks his wrist watch. "Now is almost seven, still early. Can you give me her address?"

"Are you crazy? It'll take you four hours by bike."

"I don't care. She needs emotional support and I want to be by her side at her hour of need." His voice is edged with concern. "I can't wait until tomorrow."

"Alright then." Suong pulls the door wider and leaves it ajar. "Her address is in my diary. Go get a pen and paper." She starts to walk to her dresser.

Ahead, the lighted front porch of a single-storey wooden house with a tarpaulin tent erected in front indicates that it belongs to Tuyet's parents. Quang slows down his motorcycle, turns into the slip road made of loose gravel and stops a few feet from the tarpaulin tent where several tables have been set up. One table is taken up by four men playing cards. Two coffins with framed photographs of the deceased are displayed in the front porch. Overhead, insects are buzzing around a fluorescent light.

Quong gets down from his motorcycle, rests it on its stand and goes to the carrier box at the back. He opens it, takes out a white lily funeral casket spray and steps to the table of gamblers as an owl hoots in the distance.

An old man swings his gaze to Quang and asks, "Are you looking for any one?"

"Tuyet, I'm a friend – Quang."

The old man gets up, walks to the front porch and hollers in the direction of the entrance, "Tuyet! Someone's looking for you." He returns to his table to continue his card game.

A few moments, Tuyet comes out of the house wearing

pajamas. The sight of her face twisted in anguish squeezes Quang's heart like a vise. "Tuyet, you have my deepest condolences." He hands her the white lilies and an envelope containing money to help defray the costs of the funeral. "How did this terrible accident happen?"

"My father was riding pillion on my husband's motorbike w-when a l-lorry swerved – " Tuyet starts to sob and moves to the altar to put the water lilies on top, with Quang following her.

When her hands are free, she wheels around, opens her arms to swallow Quang in a hug, collapsing against his chest as heart-wrenching sobs shake her tall frame. When her tears stop flowing, she lifts her head to look up at him. "I –I love you too, Quang, but I could not bring myself to say it to you that night." Her breath comes in sputters. "Now you know why."

"Please save your explanation for later." Quang's voice is as tender as the look in his eyes. "I'll stay here until the funeral is over. I can sleep on the floor under the porch or anywhere. Then we'll return to Saigon together."

Tuyet spears the last spring roll on the platter with a fork. "A year later, Quang and I got married." She bites the spring roll in half and puts the fork down on a small plate in front of her. "His motorbike trip to my village convinced me that he was in love with me and I was touched. When he returned to Saigon, he was sacked from his job for being absent without leave. So he became a full-time massage boy."

I nod. "That's a wonderful love story." I slurp my soup. "Wow, this soup's excellent! What soup is this?"

"Dog meat soup." Her voice is non-chalant.

"What! Pooey!" My stomach roils and I almost puke.

*   *   *

Harold (a pseudonym), aged sixty and a first-timer to Saigon, lumbers into Jezebel Bar (not its real name) in Bui Vien Street and strides to a table. The stool wobbles as he plonks his pear-shaped body on it. A waitress – her torso swallowed up in a skin-tight sequined top – hands him a one-sheet laminated menu. He orders a beer and swivels on his stool to gaze at four ladies sitting alone separately. About five or six patrons with arms draped over the shoulders of dolled-up lasses are scattered at other tables at the bar counter. The small dance floor is filled with men and women gyrating to Vietnamese pop music.

Harold assesses the four separate floozies through pouched eyes. A cute bob-haired girl garbed in a pencil skirt revealing her curves sends a tingle down his crotch. He smiles at her but she does not notice and continues to fiddle with her mobile phone held in both hands.

A waitress brings Harold his stein of beer and a small chit and deposits them on the table. "Thanks." He flicks his gaze at the chit, wrestles his wallet from his back pocket and pays her. "Keep the change." As the waitress leaves, he continues to stare at the bob-haired girl, fire licking at his loins as he popped a Viagra pill half an hour ago. *I better book her first before someone else does.*

Harold grabs his stein, rises and saunters to the bob-haired girl's table. "Hello, can I buy you a drink?" His wide mouth opens to reveal yellow teeth.

A smile nudges the edges of the girl's lips. "Where are you from?" Her milky fleshy cheeks frame a small nose and her full lips are painted a shiny pink.

Harold settles down on a stool. "New Zealand." He takes

out a handkerchief and dabs sweat off his half-bald head.

A flicker of curiosity glints in the girl's eyes. "First time in Saigon?"

"Yes, I just got here yesterday." He extends a mottled hand which she grasps lightly. "I'm Harold." He pauses. "How much?"

The girl's thick-lashed eyes beam an enquiring gaze. "Short time or overnight?"

"Overnight." Harold swipes his thin lips with his tongue.

"Barfine is five hundred thousand, service fee is three million dong.

"Too expensive."

"Why too expensive?" The girl crimps her brows. "You said you just got here yesterday. So, how many girls have you barfined out?"

A wry smile hovers on Harold's lips. "How about short time?"

The girl jolts upright. "Two million as service fee, barfine's still the same." She flutters her fake long eye-lashes. "You'll be my first customer, darling."

"Okay, deal."

The girl stretches out a dainty hand with fingers wearing pink varnish. "Please give me the barfine now." She locks her gaze with his for a moment. "I need to pay my mamasan." Her eyes cast downward at the mug. "When you finish your beer, we can leave."

Harold wrenches his wallet from his back pocket and counts out the amount. "Here, you are." He hands over the cash.

The girl takes the money and holds it in her hand. "Excuse me, I'll go pay my mamasan now." She gives his arm a fleeting tender grasp. "I'll be back." She climbs down from the stool, heads towards the dance floor and squeezes through gaps in the mass of bodies before disappearing.

Fifteen minutes roll away to bass riffs reverberating in the air. Impatience gnaws at Harold's gut and his bulgy eyes span wider to search for his "girlfriend" in the hall. But she is nowhere to be seen. He empties his mug, slams it on the table with a gush of frustration rolling from his lips and strides towards the bar. "Hey, bartender, can I talk to the mamasan?"

The balding barman scrunches his face. "Why?" His voice is like a low growl from a dog with bronchitis.

Harold stands with both feet slightly apart, placing both palms on the counter. "I just barfined a bargirl – err, damn, I didn't even ask for her name – paid her some money and now she's disappeared."

"We don't have a mamasan, mister. This is a freelancer bar, you understand?"

"Shit! I've been scammed!"

The barman gives a sad shake of his head. "Better luck next time."

"But why didn't she want my business? It could have been a bigger amount."

"For some men," says the bartender, scrutinizing Harold's toad-like face, "*Beauty and the Beast* can come true in real life, but for her anyway, it only exists in the movies."

Heat crawls up the back of Harold's neck as the innuendo of the statement ripples through him.

* * *

Thirty-three-year-old Clement Chu (a pseudonym), hailing from

Kuala Lumpur, tosses his mike on the empty seat on his right, turns and leans to kiss his hostess Mai on the cheek. "Can I have happy ending before I leave, darling?"

"What? You're leaving after only one hour?"

My wife will be back in the hotel from her shopping soon. "My friends are waiting for me to take dinner."

"Happy ending is four million." Mai hikes a thumb at the ensuite bathroom. "We can do it in there." She smiles, revealing perfect teeth. "Can you pay first?"

Clement and Mai are in a posh KTV room of Bonanza KTV Nightclub (name changed), which is fitted with chandeliers and ersatz King Louis XVI furniture. Earlier, during the lineup of six hostesses, tall-and-big-boned Mai dropped one shoulder strap of her loose-fitting top to reveal a big round breast. "Just giving you a peek of something you like very much," she purred in a husky voice. Clement's groin clenched. "I take her!" he said to the mamasan, garbed in a knee-length tux dress.

Now in the bathroom, a nude Clement is sitting on the plastic seat-cover of the toilet bowl. Joined to him, Mai is bouncing up and down, her back facing him, her bare feet resting on his thighs. The seat cover squeaks like a Vietnamese bamboo rat being roasted alive. Clement rolls his eyes up to heaven as he squeezes Mai's breasts.

Minutes stretch by. "Stop!" croaks Clement. "Stop! Stop!"

"Why?" Mai's voice is a hushed gasp.

"The seat cover's brittle, it may break! Stop, please!"

"I can't! I'm coming!" Mai bounces harder, her thigh muscles cording with the effort. "I'm coming! I'm coming!" She bounces harder still. "Ooooh… Ahhhhh… Tsssssssk….."

Crack! The seat-cover splits into three pieces and slips off the toilet bowl. Clement falls butt first inside the bowl. "Eeeeeek!" he shrieks, grabbing the sides of the toilet bowl.

Like a cat, Mai leaps away from Clement, landing with both feet on the marble floor. She turns to face Clement. "Darling, let me help you out." She stretches out her hands for Clement to hold.

As Clement is pulled to his feet, he says, "Please ask for my bill."

Later, the mamasan places a silver platter containing the bill in front of Clement and when he sees the first figure his jaw drops. "What! Minimum spend is four million dong? No one told me!" His tone of voice drips with ire.

The erstwhile friendly Mamasan scowls, picks up the menu and shoves it in Clement's face. "See?" She points to the bottom of the first page. "It's in small print at the bottom. Minimum spend is imposed on Friday and Saturday." She tosses the menu with disdain on the coffee table.

Dammit! I didn't see it! Clement re-looks the bill. *Sweet suffering saints! Cost of seat-cover is five hundred thousand dong! There's also mandatory tip for mamasan, mandatory tip for hostess, forty thousand for a glass of plain water and fifty thousand for two face towels I never asked for. Also a 15% service charge. Even without minimum spend, this place is a rip-off!* He wrestles his wallet from his trouser pocket, counts some money notes and tosses them on the silver platter.

The door swings open. Six toughies wearing black t-shirts with the word "SECURITY" in white troop in. As Mummy leaves the room, they surround Clement, whose eyes span wider in shock.

"Goodnight darling!" Mai rises from the sofa. "Bye-bye!"

She squeezes between a gap in the men and leaves the room.

A bulldog-faced man thrusts out his grubby paw. "Tip, sir?" When Clement remains silent and still for a moment, he repeats in an edgy voice, an octave louder, "My tip, sir?" Then he utters something in Vietnamese language to the other men and they come alive with sinister-sounding mutters, their faces turning hostile, their eyes sparking fire.

Clement's knees start to flutter. *WTF, I better pay to get out in one piece!* He tips the six bouncers and recalls, albeit too late, what his tourist guide said earlier, "For cheap KTVs, go to those in Chinatown."

* * *

Sitting inside the living room of his condominium, Masaki Takizawa (not his real name) aims the remote control at the TV and presses a button to switch it off. He rises from his armchair and saunters across the living room into the kitchen. Inside, his wife Fumiko, donned in an apron over a beige sheath dress, is standing by the stove, frying eels on a pan.

Masaki moves to his wife's side and lifts the lid off a pot of miso soup sitting on a grate next to the frying pan. "I'll scoop the soup into bowls," he says to his wife and reaching out for a bowl on a shelf.

Fumiko turns off the gas burner. "The eels are ready." She flips the strips of fish on a plate and, at that moment, the doorbell in the living room rings.

"Ah, that must be my *giao-vien,*" says Masaki with a chortle. "*Giao vien* means teacher!" He transfers three bowls of miso soup on a tray and takes them to the dining room.

Masaki Takizawa, aged thirty-three, is an engineering manager of a Japanese-Vietnamese joint-venture manufacturing company in Vinh Loc Industrial Park, HCM City. A week ago, he told his wife Fumiko that he has enrolled for Vietnamese language lessons and has invited his teacher for dinner.

From the dining room, Masaki goes to the wooden front door and opens it. "Good evening, *giao-vien* Hiep," he greets, his angular face cracking into a big smile. "Please come in."

Standing a few feet behind him, Fumiko cocks her head to look at Hiep in the doorway. Short, squat and possibly in her early forties, Hiep has on a tight dress cinching at her broad waist, making her breasts look big, and she wears her hair in a bob with bangs. Her features are prominent, without make-up, and her sharp big eyes and thick brows seem to express masculine daring. A tote bag hangs from her right shoulder.

"Same to you, Masaki – if I may address you that way?" Hiep slips off her sandals, leaves them outside the doorway and saunters in, stopping a few feet from Fumiko.

"Fumiko," says Masaki, casting a side glance at his wife, "this is my language teacher Miss Hiep Thien. She's from Pearl River Language School." Then he moves to the doorway to close the wooden door.

"Hello, Fumiko!" Smiling, Hiep slips her tote bag off her shoulder and dips a pudgy hand inside. "How are you adjusting to life in Ho Chi Minh City?" She pulls out a cardboard box measuring three inches by fourteen inches.

"I quite like the slower pace of life here as compared to Tokyo."

"Excuse me," says Masaki as he starts to walk away. "I'll go take out the cold dishes from the fridge."

Hiep passes the package to Fumiko. "Here's a small souvenir for you." She hitches the tote bag back on her right shoulder.

"Oh! Thank you!" Fumiko curves her lips upward, her almond-shaped eyes crinkling at the corners. Can I open it?"

"Of course."

Fumiko opens the cardboard box at one end and pulls out a folded fan together with a lacquered wooden stand. "Oh, what a beautiful fan! And there's a stand to display it too." Smiling, she starts to move away. "Come, let's go to the dining room."

Seated at the dining table, Hiep grips a piece of fried eel from a platter with her chopsticks and brings it to her mouth. "You've a fine husband who dedicated to his career," she says to Fumiko sitting across her. "He told me his job as engineering manager involves supervising several Vietnamese technicians who are not fluent in English. So that's why he's taking Vietnamese lessons to communicate better with them." She puts her chopsticks down and wipes her upper lip with her tongue. "Because he's learning business Vietnamese, not every-day Vietnamese, his lessons with me are one-on-one."

Fumiko nods in understanding. "Yes, he told me his lessons will be Monday, Wednesday and Friday evening. When he has mastered the language, perhaps he can teach me."

Hiep takes a spoon and slurps some miso soup from a small bowl in front of her. "I'm sure he'll get a promotion soon."

Seated beside Fumiko, Masaki responds in jest, "A promotion will help me to recoup my investment in tuition fees!"

The trio laughs heartily and continues to eat.

A fortnight later...

Fumiko picks up a pair of her husband's trousers from the laundry basket and dips her hand inside the right pocket. It's empty. She checks the right pocket and finds a few facial-tissue wads inside. Taking the wads out, she tosses the pair of trousers into the tub of the washing machine beside her. Next to go inside are two of her used panties and bras and a t-shirt.

Now she lifts up a white shirt and a faint whiff of fragrance teases her nostrils. *Eh? Perfume? Where did it come from? Maybe from me when I hugged him?* Casting the white shirt at her feet, she rummages through the other clothes and pulls out a checked shirt. Holding the checked shirt near to her nose, she takes a sniff but the fragrance of perfume is absent. She returns the checked shirt to the laundry basket and picks out a pair of white briefs. Turning it inside out, she examines it closely. Her eyebrows crimp with concern. *Looks like a small patch of stain, possibly seminal stain.* She dumps the contents of laundry basket, including the briefs, into the washing machine and closes the lid.

Now, she picks up the white shirt, shuffles on slippers to the bedroom and sits at the dresser. She sniffs the shirt again, drops it on her lap and one by one, she opens her perfume bottles and smells every bottle to compare if any of the fragrances match that on the shirt. She tested six bottles. *The perfume doesn't seem to be mine. Did the perfume come from another woman?*

Fumiko returns to the washing machine, tosses the shirt inside and switches the machine on. *Is that woman Hiep Thien really a teacher?* She goes to sit on the settee in the living room and picks up her smart phone on the coffee table. Tapping the screen of the phone, she searches for Pearl River Language School on Google, gets its phone number and calls.

"Hello? Is this Pearl River Language School?"

"Yes," says a female voice. "How can I help you?"

"Do you have a teacher called Hiep Thien?"

"Yes, we do, but Miss Hiep Thien is having a class now."

Hmm...she's really a teacher. "Oh, never mind then, thank you."

Fumiko ends the call, leans back in her seat and her eyes trail into a vacant stare, her mind scrambling for possibilities of how her husband's shirt caught the smell of perfume.

Masaki steps out of the en-suite bathroom into the master bedroom in a loose pajama shirt and long pants. Dried by the bathroom hair dryer, his hair is a dark, shiny, fluffy carpet on his head and his breath smells of mint from toothpaste. As he moves toward the wall switch to tap off the ceiling lights, Fumiko, lying on the bed, reaches out for the chain of the side lamp and pulls it. The light snaps on, casting a yellowish circle around the side table, which instantly turns brighter and bigger as the ceiling lights go off.

Masaki lies down on his back beside Fumiko, his eyes looking at the ceiling for a few moments before closing. A hint of perfume comes floating from Fumiko, dressed in a baby-doll silk lingerie, exposing cleavage and milky thighs, her hair spread across her pillow.

Fumiko inches towards him. "Darling, I want to make love." Her hand slides beneath the elastic waist band of his pajama pants down to his belly and penis. *Sheesh! It's limp like tofu! Must have fucked before coming home!* She starts to squeeze his penis.

Masaki holds her wrist and pulls her hand away. "Aww...not tonight, dear, I'm tired." His voice is a half-groan.

Fumiko sits up, her eyes flashing anger. "I've noticed that you can't make love with me after going for lessons. Are you visiting prostitutes?"

"Of course not!" Masaki pushes himself up to a sitting position. "I come home straight from school every time, and tonight I'm tired." His eyes blink a few times, as if begging her to understand.

"Are you fucking Miss Hiep Thien in the classroom?"

"What!" Masaki's jaw drops. "How can you even think of that? Have you been watching too much porn! My goodness, you think I've such poor taste in women?" He pauses. "This weekend –" the tone of his voice suddenly softens to match the look in his eyes "—we'll go to a wellness spa, take a couple's package and spend some quality time together, okay?" He places an arm across her chest to push her backward on the bed. "Now, please, let's get some sleep."

Motorcycle-taxi rider Duong stares at the open gates of the factory across the road from behind a tree. Two days ago, he was introduced to Mrs. Fumiko Takizawa by his friend who works as a security guard at the condominium where she lives. At the meeting, Duong was hired by her to tail her husband from his factory after work on Monday, Wednesday and Friday. Today is his first surveillance on the subject.

Now, he sees a Honda Jazz bearing the registration number given to him by Mrs. Fumiko Takizawa leaving the open gates of the factory. He dashes to his motorcycle parked a few feet away, kick-starts the engine and speeds off to follow the car.

Forty-five minutes later, the Honda Jazz reaches Le Thanh Ton Street in Little Japan and swerves into a side road. The car slows down as the driver searches for a parking bay. He finds one, parks the car and gets out. The driver walks back to Le

Thanh Ton Street, and Duong tails him on his motorbike at a discreet distance. When he enters a bar, Duong stops and parks his motorbike further ahead. He fishes out his mobile phone from his pocket.

"Hello? Fumiko?" Duong starts to walk on the pavement towards the bar. "I am Duong." He stops a few feet away from the bar entrance where a bouncer and two promotional girls in miniskirts are stationed. "Your husband has gone inside Tsubaki Bar & Karaoke (not its real name), Le Thanh Ton Street, District One." He turns to look at the traffic when he realizes that the promotional girls have noticed him.

"Wait for me there!" Her voice is firm and determined. "I'm coming by taxi!"

Dressed in pants and blouse, Fumiko gets out of the taxi and strides towards Duong in flats, her feet kicking up dust in rage.

"Is my husband still inside?"

"I did not see him come out."

"I am going inside – please accompany me."

"Fumiko, you better not create a scene inside. They will throw you out!"

"Don't worry, I know what to say."

Fumiko and Duong step into the doorway and enter a foyer where a girl wearing a Mickey Mouse-ear hair band is stationed behind a large reception desk. "I'm looking for Masaki Takizawa," Fumiko says.

The receptionist's baby-doll face creases in puzzlement. "Madam? Yes?"

"I say I'm looking for Mr. Masaki Takizawa – he's my friend."

"Do you know which KTV room?"

"I don't know, but he invited me to join him."

"Oh?"The receptionist bites her lower lip. "Please wait here, I'll get Mummy." She turns, takes short strides on heels to enter a curtained doorway.

Moments later, a short stocky woman with a bob hair-do steps into the foyer together the receptionist.

"It's you!" Fumiko flinches as she recognizes the woman as Hiep Thien. "Your real name isn't Hiep Thien, is it?" She parks both hands on her hips.

"No, I'm Mummy Huyen." Mummy grins a shit-eating grin.

"Well, well, well, what a well-planned deception." Fumiko's voice drips with ire.

"Your husband knew you might call the school to check so he asked me to use the name of a teacher in that school." Mummy returns Fumiko's pointed stare without flinching. "What I did was requested by him in return for guaranteed business and a big tip. He has pre-booked my hostesses every Monday, Wednesday and Friday for this entire month and for next month – even paid a fat deposit. That's why he needs an excuse to go home late."

Mummy's earlier lies echo in Fumiko's mind, slicing her gut. "You bitch!"

A week later...

"*Danh gia hieu suat* means 'performance appraisal'," says silver-haired Giang, pointing at the Vietnamese words on a booklet in front of Masaki. "*Danh-gia- hieu-suat.*"

Sitting beside Giang at the dining table, Masaki repeats the phrase, "*Danh gia hieu suat, danh gia hieu suat, danh gia hieu suat* – performance appraisal." The tone of his voice is sombre.

Giang strokes his white walrus moustache with his thumb

and forefinger. "Excellent! Now let's go to the next phrase."

Giang, a retired school teacher, has been hand-picked by Fumiko to tutor Masaki business Vietnamese at home.

* * *

1977, Re-education Camp No 8, five miles north of Saigon

Fifty pairs of feet shod in flip-flop sandals slap against a grey cement floor as they walk into a hall constructed of planks and a rusty zinc roof which is supported by six wooden pillars. All the sandals were made by the owners of the feet themselves from the rubber tubes and bald tyres of left-behind American jeeps. The feet lead upward to calves of which many carry scars from old mosquito bites or from former scabies rashes or from cuts and scratches that have healed. The owners of the calves – women in their twenties and early thirties – form several rows facing a square wooden dais. Pham Linh, aged twenty-nine, wearing a loose tunic and baggy pants, is standing among other women in the front row.

A pair of feet wrapped in canvas shoes enters the hall and steps up to the dais. The feet belong to a forty-something-year-old woman with a narrow forehead and thin, mean and hard lips. She is donned in a pair of khaki pants and a short-sleeved shirt with flap pockets and epaulets. Her right hand hanging down at her side is carrying a stout rattan cane about two feet long.

"*Chao buoi sang* [Good morning], Wardress Ngon!" greet the women.

Wardress Ngon flicks her gaze across the faces of her charges. "Inmates, today will be your day of release! Congratulations on completing your re-education programme." She tucks her rattan cane under her left armpit. "Many of you have undergone personal, if not painful, transformation for the better. So, let me quote a poem written by our Founding Father Ho Chi Minh." She takes a deep breath and releases it. "*How much the rice must suffer under the pestle! But after the pounding, it comes out white like cotton! The same thing often happens to men in this world! Misfortune's workshop turns them into polished jade!*" She shifts her weight to one leg. "Of course, this change applies to women as well! All of you have become polished jade!" Her thin lips inch into a half smile which never fully forms. "Now, the final formality in your re-education is getting married to good husbands. So, we have arranged a meet-and-register session. A marriage registrar and your future husbands are waiting in the next building – Block C." She pauses for a moment at seeing the many faces that have turned sullen. "They are all former soldiers of the People's Army of Vietnam. All of them are gainfully employed. Just to remind you how lucky you are–" she raises her voice to stress her point "–currently, we have three million people unemployed and one million widows. These men fought hard in the 'Resistance War Against America' and as a reward, our grateful government has arranged them to be married to good women like you." She directs a hand to a side doorway. "Come, follow me to Block C."

Trailing behind Wardress Ngon, Linh and the other inmates troop in a single file out of the hall and traipse along a short pebble-strewn path between vegetable plots. All around them are four barbed-wire fences rising fifteen feet high, which encloses an area the size of two football fields and beyond the wire fences are thick jungles. The morning sun – round and large – throws their shadows broad and long as they enter another wooden building.

Inside, seated on rows of benches at one end of the hall are men in their twenties and early thirties, all togged up in peasant's clothes. They start to talk in hushed voices when they see the women enter. Linh flicks a quick gaze at the men and her jaw drops, his eyes spanning wider. *Oh Lord Buddha, this is a nightmare!* Murmurs and a few muffled shrieks arise from the other women.

Wardress Ngon leads the women to a cluster of stools placed at the other end of the hall. "Ladies! Sit down!" Then she moves away to stand a few feet away from a wooden desk in the centre of the hall where a plump woman with a pair of cat eye spectacles perched on her nose is seated. In front of her on the wooden desk is a book opened flat.

Linh plunks down on a stool and scans the first row of men, about thirty feet away, one by one. *The first guy has only one leg.* A chill travels down her spine. *The second man has his face and neck scarred from burns – possibly a victim of a flamethrower. The next fellow is an arm amputee. The man next to him has lost his left hand. The man beside him is wearing an eye patch and, my goodness, also missing an ear. All these men are maimed.*

Wardress Ngon casts her attention at the women, her right hand tapping the rattan cane against the side of her trousers. "When the marriage registrar calls your name and your husband-to-be's name –" she flicks her gaze at the men on the other side "– both of you go to her desk to sign your marriage documents. After this registration session, we'll have a farewell lunch in the canteen. Then you are free to go with your new-found husbands."

The marriage registrar looks down at her book and adjusts her spectacles. "First couple, Minh Ly and Lam Lap!" She flicks her gaze left and then right.

Linh hears a muffled sob as Minh Ly gets up, strides to the

registrar's desk and sits down on one of two stools provided. Lam Lap – who turns out to be a man with only one arm – lumbers with a limp to sit next to his wife-to-be.

"Newly married couples can go sit anywhere," says Wardress Ngon as the duo take turns to sign their names on the marriage documents.

Linh slumps forward – her face buried in her hands – and shuts her eyes. A silent groan rises in her chest and her heart constricts at the thought of being forced into wedlock. As she waits for the dreaded moment, the registrar calls out several pairs of names consecutively.

Then: "Pham Linh and Le Van-Huu!"

Linh's heart almost thuds to a dead stop as she looks up, her palms sticky with sweat. She rises on trembling knees and goes to sit on one of two stools at the registrar's desk. From the corner of her eye, she sees Le Van-Huu hobbling on his right leg with the help of a pair of crutches towards her. *My goodness, his left leg has been amputated below the knee!* Probably in his late twenties, Van-Huu plops clumsily on the stool and leans his crutches against the registrar's desk. He turns his pockmarked face sideways to Linh, and his thick lips part in a happy smile to reveal two missing front teeth.

Re-education Camp No 8, a year earlier

The rays of the morning sun slant in through the windows, illuminating motes floating in the cool air inside the hall. Pham Linh and forty-nine other women are standing at attention as they wait for a cue from Wardress Ngon to sing the national anthem. This singing marks the start of the inmates' daily schedule after a breakfast of gruel and steamed tapioca roots in the canteen.

Standing behind a desk placed atop a square wooden dais, Wardress Ngon waves her forefinger and hollers, "One, two, three!"

Everyone in the wooden hall sings in chorus,

"Soldiers of Vietnam, we go forward
With the one will to save our Fatherland
Our hurried steps are sounding
On the long and arduous road
Our flag, red with the blood of victory
Bears the spirit of our country
The distant rumbling of our guns
Passes over the bodies of our foes
The path to glory is built
By the bodies of our foes
Overcoming all hardships
Together we build resistance bases
Ceaselessly, for the People's cause
Let us struggle
Let us hasten to the battlefield
Onward! All together advancing
For one eternal Vietnam…"

"Alright, be seated." Wardress Ngon pulls out a rattan chair, settles down behind the desk and flips open a small book. "Today's lecture is on the pursuit of wealth in capitalism. According to Karl Marx and Friedrich Engels, the founders of Communist ideology, one major flaw of this system is that it makes the rich richer and the poor poorer. In a capitalistic economy, society is divided into two classes. First, there are those who control or have ownership of land, factories and machinery. They are called the bourgeoisie. Then, there are those who sell labour for minimal wages. They are called the proletariat or workers...." Half an hour later, Wardress Ngon snaps the book shut. "So, that ends my lecture this morning. Tomorrow, we'll look at the role of the media in a capitalistic culture." From the corner of her eye, she sees Field Wardress Loan and other female guards waiting outside at the side entrance. "Now, it's time for constructive labour. Dismiss!"

Linh and the other women march out of the hall to a nearby shed to collect their gardening tools, with Field Wardress Loan and her female guards escorting them. Then the inmates are marched to an area where *rao muong* [water spinach], *bap cai* [cabbage] and *su hao* [kohlrabi] are growing on rows of bunds. Linh and several other women are assigned the task of weeding the bunds; others will build new bunds to grow more veggies; and still others will draw water from a man-made well to water the plants.

Linh squats down in a trough between two bunds where *rao muong* is grown, digs her trowel to unearth a weed with its roots intact and pulls it out. Moving on her haunches, she works from left to right. Half an hour later, a fellow inmate calls out to her from a bund behind her, "Psst, there's a rat nest. If we can catch a few rats, we'll have a feast tonight."

Linh tosses a gaze over her shoulder. "Where?"

"There...over there." The woman points to her far right where a clump of weeds are growing in a broken section of a bund. Linh gets up, steps over a bund and stoops to check the spot which has a small burrowed hole. *Whack!* A heavy rattan cane lands on Linh's back! Pain explodes at the spot where she was hit, and her face twists in agony.

"Get back to work!" A female guard raises her rattan cane above her shoulders and gloats.

Saigon, late 1975

Several loud raps on the wooden door of her bedroom arouse Pham Linh from her sleep. She blinks, turns her face toward the door and sees a band of light at its bottom. The knocking is repeated and this time it is louder. Yawning, Linh gets out of bed, scurries to the door and opens it a crack.

The ashen face of Madam Hue, her silver-haired landlady, appears in the gap of the door. "Linh! There are some people looking for you!"

"Huh?" Linh rubs her eyes. "Who?"

"They say they're from the Department of Social Affairs. They're waiting outside." Madam Hue turns and starts to move away. "Better see what they want."

Linh follows her landlady along the outside corridor to cross the hallway where a grandfather clock on one wall shows 1:20 a.m. Linh moves to the front doorway where the iron grille door is still locked and stops a few feet away. A jimberjawed woman and a man sporting a penitentiary haircut are standing outside under the front porch. A pistol in a dark holster dangles from the belt of the man. On the roadside is the dark shape of a truck, its engine rumbling, its headlights throwing two shafts of light on the stretch of road ahead, pockmarked with tar-filled scars.

Her hair tied up in a bun, the woman – probably forty-something in age and wearing a military-style khaki uniform – plucks out a rusting badge from her shirt pocket and shows it to Linh. "I'm from the Department of Social Affairs." Her voice sounds like the caw of a crow. "Are you Pham Linh?"

"Yes, I am." Linh's brows squish in puzzlement.

"You've been identified as a former bargirl of the now-closed Dixie Bar, previously located in Bui Vien Street." Spittle sprays from the official's mouth as she speaks. "You've also bore a child to an American G.I. – a child with no last name. These are serious offences." Her voice becomes an octave louder. "We've to take you for interrogation and to be sent to a re-education camp for moral and political rehabilitation." The woman tosses her gaze to Madam Hue. "Now, open the grille door, Madam!"

Madam Hue dips a trembling hand into a side pocket of her tunic, fishes out a key and opens the door.

The official and her companion enter the hall and escort Linh outside to the waiting truck. "Go sit at the back," hollers the man.

Linh climbs up the metal steps and climbs aboard where four women and another man are seated on two separate benches on each side. After Linh plops down, the man pulls up the tailgate. The official goes to sit in the front cabin beside the driver, and the man who was earlier with her climbs into the back.

Linh overhears the driver in the front cabin ask, "Where to next?"

"Hien Cuc's home in Dinh Chieh Road." The voice belongs to the woman with the protruding jaw. "She's a former prostitute in a brothel which fronted as Viet Pussy Massage Centre – it's now a pile of rubble. After that, we've to pick up another former bargirl in Le Lai Alley. Come on, let's go!"

With a growl, the truck rumbles away.

Saigon, March 1973
The telephone at one end of the bar rings and the rough-faced

bartender steps from his spot where he is standing to answer it. It is early afternoon and there are no customers as yet and several bargirls are lounging on settees, powdering their faces and applying lip stick.

"Good afternoon! Dixie Bar." The bartender pauses. "Linh! Phone call for you! It's your boyfriend Todd!" He leaves the receiver on the bar and returns to his former spot to continue drying glasses with a terry cloth towel.

Linh gets up from her chair at a nearby table, patters on heels to the bar and lifts the receiver to her ear. "Hello, darling!" Her face is bright and her eyes brim with happiness.

"Linh! I don't know how to say this to you but I've bad news for us. U.S. troops are withdrawing from Nam. I've got to board a military plane now."

"What!" *Oh goodness, they're abandoning us!* A scowl seizes Linh's face.

"Please take care of our daughter." Todd's words sound nasal and water-logged. "I'll be back, I promise! As soon as I can!" His voice is now on the verge of cracking. "Now, you try to get out of Saigon, okay? I don't think your boys can hold back the Commies when they attack. And I'm sure they'll attack very soon. Bye, bye darling. I love you!" *Click!* The line goes dead.

Saigon, 1972

Inside Dixie Bar, sixteen pairs of feet encased in loafers, blue suede shoes, pumps, kitten-heel sandals and flats are shuffling on the scratched cement floor in a slow dance. They belong to the American combat troops on leave and the bargirls. The floor is littered with Marlboro cigarette butts, Razzles chewing gum wrappers and beer can tabs. A jukebox in a corner is playing

Simon & Garfunkel's *Bridge Over Troubled Water*, and the smoky air is laced with the stale stench of alcohol.

But not all feet are dancing. Wrapped in open-toed sandals, two feet with their ankles crossed are tucked under a round table. The feet lead up to slender calves and onward to shapely, smooth and creamy thighs exposed under the hem of a mini skirt. "Todd darling, I'm pregnant!" says the owner of the legs, Pham Linh, whose mini skirt leads upward to a cotton top from which a pair of voluptuous breasts peek from under a V-neckline.

Planted firmly on the floor across the open-toed sandals is a pair of deerskin moccasins, spaced about two feet apart. "Wow! That's great news! It'll be wonderful to have someone calling me 'Daddy' soon," says the wearer of the moccasins, twenty-four-year-old American G.I. Todd Johnson (not his real name). As he speaks, his gaze traces Linh's high cheekbones, her full lips and the graceful curve of her neck plunging down to a deep décolletage. "How many months?"

"Two."

"Worry not, darling." He rests a hairy hand on Linh's arm on the table and squeezes it. "I'll send you money every month as child maintenance."

Back to the present...
"So, that's the story of my mother, Pham Linh," says Mummy Yen, pressing her lips into a firm line. "After the war, all former bargirls were detained for re-education and later forced to marry North Vietnamese soldiers who were maimed." Already in her late forties, Mummy is togged up in black legging pants and a carrot-hued flowing blouse.

Sitting opposite her across a glass-topped table, I take a glug of whisky from my shot glass, emptying it. "How do you know her story?" The whisky lubes my throat and I release an exhale.

Mummy Yen and I toss our gazes at the trumpet player on stage who has risen to play a melody in solo, and then she and I lock gazes again.

"How do you know her story?"

"Her parents were allowed visits when she was under re-education. They told me."

I point at my shot glass. "What about you? I mean, who raised you?"

Mummy Yen grabs the whisky bottle at her side and refills my shot glass halfway. "My mother gave me up for adoption and I grew up in a farm. After her release, she discreetly visited me whenever she had an opportunity and I was told she was my auntie." Mummy replaces the whisky bottle on its former spot. "One day, when I was ten or eleven, my mother's handicapped husband tailed her to the farm on his three-wheeled motorbike." Mummy takes a pair of tongs, picks up two ice cubes from a container and drops them in my shot glass. "When he saw my mother with me, he hobbled on one leg and thrashed her with one crutch. He even wanted to kill me but spared my life after pleading from my step-parents. That was my mother's last visit to me. I worked on the farm for many years. The launch of *Doi Moi* in the late nineties saw many bars and nightclubs coming up in Saigon. So, I left the farm and started working in one bar after another."

"Why didn't you go to America when you were younger?"

"You tell me. How?"

Flummoxed, I scratch the back of my head and gaze into my whisky.

10

Kuala Lumpur Mishmash

The silvery curtain at the stage parts and shafts of orange-hued lights from the ceiling reveal a man seated behind an electronic organ. "Good evening everybody!" he blasts into the microphone at his side. "Clap your hands! You're looking good!" The crowd whoops and he starts to sing, *"Come on let's twist again... Like we did last summer!.."*

I am sitting at a first-row table in One-Stop Food Court, Gelang Road, with a plate of golden brown chicken wings in front of me. Smells of cooked food, alcohol and sweaty bodies sting my nostrils. Saturday evening is a full house here because of the performance by professional singers.

Several pairs of women and men flutter to the empty space in front of the stage, their faces plastered with smiles. Arms hanging in front, they twist their hips, bending their knees, and occasionally executing back-heel kicks.

Among the dancers is an overweight man in his forties with strands of hair slicked on his balding scalp with pomade. Face flushed from alcohol, he is partnered with a pear-shaped China doll with piggy-podgy eyes. The butterball has a beer belly hanging over his unbuckled belt that is barely holding up his pants which is worn several inches below his hips. I reckon he went to the toilet earlier and forgot to buckle his belt when he came out.

"Yeaaah, let's twist again... Like we did last year!"

The singer yells, jabs a finger in the air. *"Who's that, flying up there? Is it a bird? Noooooo…"*

In the midst of rocking her body, the China doll points to the roly-poly's crotch. "Your bird! Your bird! Your bird!"

His pants are slipping below his bulging crotch! He continues to twist his hips to the rhythm of the song.

"Is it a plane? Noooooooo…Is it the twister? Yeaaaah!"

Looking up, the man directs a pudgy finger at the ceiling and executes a vicious twist with his booty.

His pants drop to his ankles! My jaw drops too!

With nary any embarrassment, he lifts his pants, buckles his belt and continues to swing until the song ends.

I lift my beer stein to take a glug only to freeze when I see a pair of shapely legs out of the corner of my eyes. I turn my head slightly for a better view and put my beer stein down.

The owner of the legs has just occupied the adjacent table to my right. My gaze travels up her shins past her stiletto straps, up her slender thighs poking out from under a red skirt, and up to her narrow hips which extend to a model-like torso wrapped in a tight top. Finally, my gaze reaches her face, framed by long straight hair. Her lined face is long, angular and has a crooked thin nose. Her small, fierce-looking eyes indicate she is not one to be doesn't messed around with. I put her age at around late thirties.

I pick up a chicken wing, tear off a piece of meat and chew.

A middle-aged john wannabe steps up to her table, pulls out a chair and sits down. "How much?"

"One hundred?'

"Eighty?"

I bring my beer stein to take a swallow.

She points at her shadow on the floor with her forefinger. "For eighty, you can fuck my shadow!"

I choke on my beer which rises to the back of my nostrils as the prospective john scuttles away.

Minutes stretch by. A man who looks like somebody's grandfather goes to sit next to her. "Price?" he asks, draping one arm over the back of her chair.

"One hundred."

"How about seventy?"

The floozy twists in her seat and grabs the oldster's crotch with one hand. "For seventy, I'll give you a hand job right here!" Eyes glinting like shards of shattered glass, she fumbles his fly for the zipper. "Come, open your pants!" Her tone of voice is edged with scorn.

Heat rushes up the back of my neck. Face turning red, Pops gets up with a screech of his chair and leaves in a hurry, his Japanese slippers flopping on the cement floor. A loud guffaw erupts from a few men occupying a nearby table.

Time passes like a legless rat crawling in the outside gutter of the food court. Up next is a rotund john who resembles a short wooden barrel. Probably in his thirties, he has a cherubic face and a double chin. I guess he weighs almost two hundred pounds. Garbed in baggy short pants, the walking barrel stands in front of the tootsie. "Your price, darling?"

I bring my beer stein to my lips and start to take a swallow.

The floozy casts her gaze from his head to his rotund frame. "How many inches is your dick?" She thrusts out her hand to flick her middle finger at his crotch. "I charge one hundred ringgit per inch!" She hikes her chin up, her lips in a half-sneer, half-smile.

Shock grabs my windpipe and I spray beer from my mouth to the table. The buttercup ambles away.

Two twenty-something-year-old lassies walk up to a man with a flat nose spread across half his broad face. The taller of the two has on a mini skirt revealing fat thighs with tattoos of cat's paws, while her timid-looking companion is sporting a cropped top revealing a chiseled abdomen.

Beaming confidence, the taller girl pushes bangs off her forehead. "Darling, want massage with happy ending?"

The prospect swings his gaze from the stage to the tall girl. "No thanks."

"Why? Am I not pretty?" She runs her fingers through her curly hair spilling over her shoulder."

The man scratches his flat nose. "No hard feelings, you're too fat."

The taller girl thrusts a hand at her bob-haired, petite companion. "How about my sister? Only twenty-three, a first-timer in this profession."

"Nope. She's inexperienced, will be like a corpse lying in bed."

The taller floozy blinks. "You want someone experienced?"

"Experience is important for good job performance."

The hussy opens her handbag, fishes out her handphone and calls a number. "Hello, Mum? Can you come to the food court? Got a potential customer here."

"Can I share your table?" asks a lean, sinewy stranger garbed in Hawaii-style shirt hanging outside his pants.

I thrust an open palm at a chair near me and he drags it out and sits down.

The female singer on stage finishes her song, takes a bow and trots off to the wing. The dancers disperse and the organist tickles away to fill the intermission.

A middle-aged China doll with fake boobs looking like a camel's humps at the adjacent table harpoons my attention. She is chatting with a man wearing salt-and-pepper hair like a hurrah's nest.

Pops asks the cherubic-faced China doll, "Can you sing China's national anthem?"

"Of course!" She leans forward and sings, *"Arise, we who refuse to be slaves;*

With our very flesh and blood, let us build our new Great Wall!

The peoples of China are at their most critical time; everybody must roar defiance…"

Squishing my eyebrows, I ask the lean, sinewy stranger sharing my table, "What's going on?"

The stranger coughs and swallows the glob of phlegm he worked up. "He's verifying her nationality."

The China doll finishes her song and she leaves with her john, tottering away with a Malacca cane walking stick.

"I can't understand local men." My table-sharer shakes his head. "They think China pussy is better than local pussy and prefer the former. Sometimes, there are local women working here – those in their forties from our local villages – who pretend to be from China. They tell fat lies that they're from a big city like Changsha or Wuhan or Hangzhou. Apparently, this ploy increases their marketability and they snare more customers." He takes a glug of his beer and wipes his mouth with his sleeve. "However, veteran whore-mongers verify their nationalities by asking them to sing China's national anthem."

A possible explanation bubbles in my mind for this attraction towards China women: the perceived exotic factor.

* * *

Inside a hotel, the Bangladeshi janitor, early twenties, glides the vacuum cleaner across the carpet in the corridor between rows of rooms. Outside a particular room, muffled groaning and loud thuds come from the thin walls. He switches off the vacuum cleaner and moves to peep in the keyhole. In the reflection of the dresser mirror, a young man is arching his back like a butterfly-stroke swimmer on the low metal bed and the pancake-thin mattress is hitting the floor repeatedly!

The head chambermaid, a portly Indonesian with hair tied up in a bun, rounds a corner and enters the corridor. "Hey! What're you doing?" she hollers, her tone of voice like that of a Mother Superior's admonishing a nun. "You must respect our guests' privacy! Or I'll report you to our GM." She saunters towards the janitor.

The Bangladeshi jerks upright and his face creases into a sheepish smile, exposing white gleaming teeth. He forms a circle with the thumb and forefinger of one hand and jabs repeatedly into it with the other forefinger. Grinning, he points at the door.

"Oh? This I must see!" The Indonesian woman moves towards the door, stoops and squints one eye to peek inside the keyhole with the other.

Inside the room that the duo peeped inside earlier, Govinda (not his real name) steps out of the en-suite bathroom and tosses the bath towel on the bed. He grabs his boxers from a hook on a wall and steps into them. "Did I make you happy?"

Standing in front of the dresser mirror, Kareena (a pseudonym) reaches behind her back to hook her black brassier. "The mattress is wet with my stains." The corners of her lips turn in a satisfied grin. "We must try studded condoms next time." She slips her top over her head, picks up her jeans from the dresser chair and wriggles into them.

Govinda slips into his pants. "For next month's appointment, can you book a hotel in another part of town? I've friends working around here and I don't want them to see me." He slips on his shirt.

"Sure." Kareena takes out some money notes from her handbag. "Here's your payment."

"Thanks." Govinda pockets the money. "Actually, what's wrong with your husband?" He pulls out a small comb from his back pocket and starts to groom his hair.

So begins Kareena's tale...

Two years ago...
A naked Kareena sits up on the bed and leans against the headboard. "Why didn't you tell me earlier?" She wraps her arms around her breasts and tucks her knees up. "You're not being fair to me!"

The side table lamp casts a shadow of Amrish in a state of nature next to Kareena. "I-I was afraid you'd leave me!" Lips quivering, he is sitting with one knee raised and the other knee bent and resting on the bed.

Kareena and Amrish are in a hotel room on their wedding night.

"Have you seen a doctor?"

"I have but I can't afford the procedure." Amrish rests one hairy hand on Kareena's knee. "We can make it together no matter what my shortcomings are, darling. With Lord Krishna as my witness, I swear I'll do my best to make you happy."

"I know you love me but I'm a normal woman – " the muscles in Kareena's throat twitch as she struggles to form the words "—w-with sexual needs."

Her words stab. "Perhaps, I'll go to a Bangkok clinic later after I've saved enough." A flicker of pain shadows Amrish's face as he releases an exhale of frustration.

Hutan Melintang fishing village, twenty-five years ago...
Five-year-old Amrish runs stark naked along the wooden pier extending over the mangrove-dotted river bank and leaps into muddy waters. "Yay!" he giggles as water splashes upward.

Carrying glass jars in their hands, his two friends are trudging on the mud flats, searching for small colourful crabs. In the mangrove trees, Blue Flycatchers and Pittas chirp and warble. "Hey, Amrish, come join us," says one of them.

Amrish moves to shallow waters by doing the dog paddle. He stands on soft earth to take a breather, wiping his face with his hands. A tortoise, the size of a dinner plate, swims towards Amrish and spots what looks like a short fat worm. With ferocity, the tortoise snaps at it!

"Aaaaargh!" Amrish clutches at his groin and comes out of the water, blood trickling between his thighs.

"Oh *Amma*!" yells one boy, face twisted in horror. "His

ankuri has been bitten off!"

Govinda chugs his beer and puts the frosted mug on the table with a thud. "Kareena has been my regular client for almost a year." He takes out a wad of tissue and wipes his lips. "We meet once a month and she also uses sex toys to masturbate."

"Oh?" My lips part in surprise. "How do you know?" I pour more beer into Govinda's mug.

"Once, she wanted to order some sex toys online but was afraid to use her name and address." Govinda's eyes brim with empathy. "So, she asked me to buy them on her behalf and I obliged."

* * *

"Line-up!" hollers the stocky Papasan, whose mean-looking face looks like it needs a shave.

Six foreign girls, all in their twenties, all wearing mini-skirts, strut out from the wings and sit on the banquette set atop the long, narrow stage, illuminated by overhead lights.

Sitting together on a settee facing the stage, fifty-year-old Lawrence (not his real name) and his son Tony (a pseudonym), aged twenty-five, lean forward, their eyes spanning wider to get a clear look of the massage ladies.

Tony wipes sweat off his brow with his sleeve. "Papa, I'm a bit nervous!"

"I've not done this since getting married to your mum." Lawrence swallows hard. "But let's get our feet wet and the next time will be a pleasure instead of pressure."

In a funeral home in KL, one month ago ...

"I've very sorry about your wife Jessica," says Mrs. Robinson as she hands a casket spray of white gladioli to Lawrence, togged up in dark clothes. "My deepest condolences to you and your family."

"Thank you for your condolences." Lawrence takes the flowers with both hands. "This was very sudden and unexpected. Jessica suffered a heart attack when doing line-dancing on Sunday. I reckon the Good Lord has urgent duties for her in Heaven."

Tony and his wife Regina step up to Mrs. Robinson. "Thank you for coming, Madam," says Tony, his voice a feeble croak.

Lawrence turns to face the trio. "Mrs. Robinson, this is my son Tony and my daughter-in-law Regina."

"How do you do?" Mrs. Robinson shakes Tony's hand. "I've known your mother many years. She played excellent bridge. She was the kindest person I've ever known. She wouldn't even dare to kill a cockroach." She flicks her gaze at Regina's baby bump. "I see both of you are going to become parents soon."

"My expected delivery date is four months' time." Regina smiles feebly. "If only my mother-in-law – " her voice trails off on a choking sob " –then s-she would be a grandmother soon."

One year ago...

Lawrence and his family are in the living room watching TV. As soon as the movie ends, Lawrence points the remote control at the TV, presses a button to change to a different channel. The prime-time news is on and images of uniformed men breaking down the doors of cubicles in a massage centre appear on the screen.

Lawrence places the remote control on his lap. "Looks like a raid on a hanky-panky spa." He squirms on the settee and the springs below squeak.

Jessica, lounging next to Lawrence, clucks her tongue. "That petite girl being led away looks very young, just out of her teens."

Lawrence scratches the back of his head. "That shophouse looks like it's in Pandan Jaya."

"Huh? How do you know?" Jessica turns her head sideways to glare at Lawrence. "You were there before?"

"Of course not! As God is my witness, I've never stepped inside those dirty places and never will."

Regina shifts in her armchair facing the TV. "Useless men!" She sneers, her lips twisted in a scowl. "They'll burn in hell for cheating on their wives."

Sitting on an ottoman next to the armchair, Tony reaches to hold his wife's hand. "They've forgotten how to fight lust with God's words."

"And what are those words, dear?" Regina's voice is honey-sweet.

Tony clears his throat and recites several verses from the Bible.

Lawrence's chest swells with pride. "Tony's a chip of the old block – a God-fearing man."

Jessica flicks her gaze to her daughter-in-law. "We're lucky to be married to good men."

* * *

Crotch bulging, Mike Mah (a pseudonym), early twenties, stares with frog-like eyes at the lasses standing on parade in front of him.

"From left to right," enthuses the balding papasan sitting next to Mike. "Lulu, Vietnam – Mandarin speaking; Qing Qing,

China, former motor-show model; Ratana, Bangkok girl, speaks Thai and English; Karawek from Chiangmai, Mandarin and Thai-speaking; last girl is Mona from Jakarta – a new car engine, first time here."

"I take Lulu." Mike flashes a grin at the papasan

"Lulu! The rest dismiss!" The papasan rises and moves away.

Lulu steps down from the stage and latches her hand on Mike's wrist. Smiling, she leads him up a staircase and they enter a dim corridor lined on both sides with cubicles. Each cubicle has a curtained entrance, no door. Midway down the corridor, she stops at a cubicle and draws the curtains apart. She steps inside with Mike following behind.

Lulu undresses and wraps a bathing tower around herself. "Come, we shower." She takes another towel from a hook on one wall and hands it to Mike, who's now in the raw.

Inside the bathroom, Lulu showers Mike from face to toes. Then she cleans herself and goes to sit on the toilet bowl. "Darling, I need to pee. But I can't do it with someone looking at me. Can you go back to the room first?"

"Sure." Mike leaves the bathroom and pulls the door shut behind him.

Shivering from the cold air, he walks down the corridor, stops outside his room and pulls the curtain apart.

"Eeeeeeek!" screams a naked woman lying on a mattress on the floor, feet in the air.

"Hoooooi!" hollers the unclad man on top of her, looking up. "Get out! Get out!" His face is screwed up from embarrassment.

"Oooops, sorry!" Mike flinches, taking a step backward. "Wrong room! I'm sorry!" He draws the curtain back.

"Next room!" hollers Lulu, stepping out of the bathroom.

"Next room further down!"

* * *

Collin Chow (not his real name), owner of Lust Valley Nightclub (name changed) in the city's Golden Triangle, guns his BMW along the deserted Cheras Road as he heads for home. His mobile phone propped upright on his car dashboard rings and the caller ID shows it's Mummy Molly.

Collin switches off his car radio and taps the screen of his mobile phone.

"Mr. Chow, did you lock the front and back doors before leaving?"

"Yes, why?"

"I'm still in the club – I heard a noise in the kitchen."

"Anyone still there?"

"Nope, everyone has left."

Collin brakes to a screeching stop at a traffic light. "Call the security office."

"What can a guard do? You've forgotten?"

"About what?"

"A year ago on *this* day, our Indonesian hostess Dayanti committed suicide because her boyfriend – he's our regular client – dumped her after making her pregnant. Today's the first anniversary of her death."

"Yes, now I remember. Dayanti jumped from the third-floor car park."

"Now the noise's coming from one of the karaoke rooms! I'm going to confront her spirit! That's the only way to get rid of her."

The traffic light turns green and Collin steps on the gas.

"Don't! Might be a burglar! Stay in your room and call security."

Silence.

"Mummy, please answer me!"

"I've found my bible. Now I'm fashioning a cross from two metal chopsticks!"

"Mummy, remain in your room, lock it! Call security!"

Silence.

"I'm on speaker mood, phone's in my pocket. I'm going out of my room now!"

Seconds pass.

"Where're you now?"

Silence for several seconds.

"*Kriiik! Kriiik! Kriiik!* Arrrrrrgh! She's behind me!"

Silence.

"Mummy! What's happening?" Sweat suddenly beads Collins's forehead. "Are you alright?" He plucks a tissue from a box and wipes his forehead. "Mummy! Answer me!"

Silence.

"Mummy, I'm coming back!"

Silence.

At the next junction, Collin executes an illegal U-turn. His BMW burns rubber on the road as he zooms back to the city, the wind whistling like a banshee through the air vents of the dashboard.

I take a glug of my Chinese tea and put the glass down. "Was it Dayanti's ghost?" I grab more noodles with my chopsticks and bring them to my mouth.

Sitting across me, Collin is picking his teeth with a toothpick. "When I reached the building, I went to the security office, got a guard to accompany me to my nightclub. The front door was still locked and I unlocked it to enter the hall. Nobody was there." He tosses the toothpick in the ashtray on the table and leans back in his chair. "One by one I checked the karaoke rooms. In one room I found Mummy Molly lying on the floor. Beside her was a cross made of two chopsticks tied at right angles by rubber bands. She had fainted. A loud *kriiik! kriiik! kriiik!* made me jump." A chortle gushes from his lips. "The security guard bolted from the room! The noise came from under the coffee table. Uttering a silent prayer, I bent on trembling knees and looked. The noise was made by a big cicada!"

"How did the cicada get inside your nightclub?"

Collin shrugs. "Possibly through the glass louvre windows in the toilet."

* * *

The staccato sound of my leather shoes thudding on the concrete pavement breaks the silence in the sidewalk as I approach the woman garbed in a saree, illuminated by street lamps and store lighting. She is standing about twenty paces away from the entrance of a budget hotel at Tuanku Abdul Rahman Road, KL.

Turning to look at me, she claps her hands. *Piak! Piak! Piak!* I stop a few feet away from her. "Is that a signal?"

"This clap means I'm a *hijra*." Her cheekbones are high, nose long and straight, and her voice reminds me of sandpaper.

I lock gazes with her, my attention focused on her eyebrows which have been shaven and re-drawn. "What's a *hijra*?"

"A transgender."

"Where're you from?"

"Tirunelveli, Tamilnadu."

"Come, we go for a drink, I pay you fifty ringgit, and we talk?"

"Okay."

"I'm Freddy," I lie, stretching out my hand.

She grips my hand loosely. "My name's Gautami."

Looking to my right, I gesture with an open palm. "There's a twenty-four-hour restaurant over there, near a side alley. "I flick my gaze back to her. "What's your real name?" I start to walk.

Gautami begins to stride beside me. "Who's your favourite Indian actor?"

I cast my gaze at two jeans-clad men strolling along the sidewalk across the road to think and then back to her. "Sanja Dutt."

Gautami releases a noisy exhale. "Then let Sanjay be my real name."

Tirunelveli, Tamilnadu, fifteen years ago…

Thirteen-year-old Sanjay opens the door of his elder sister's bedroom and enters. He steps to the closet and opens it. A row of dresses, sarees, and skirts steals his breath away. Face glowing with excitement, he undresses. From the closet, he takes out a dirndl skirt, puts it on and stands in front of the dresser mirror to admire himself. He steps back to the closet, takes out a pair of kitten-heels and steps into them.

Sanjay hears the sound of harsh air sucked through gritted teeth, a grunt and the swish of an arm swinging through the air. *Thwack!* From behind, a palm lands on the side of his head. He falls sideways to the floor, his head spinning for a moment.

His father, Vishal (not his real name), grabs him by his upper arms and jerks him to a standing position. "Sanjay! Don't play with girls' clothes! Understand?"

"But– but I like– "

"No, buts!" Vishal's eyes glint with fury. "Go to your room to study!"

Five years later ...

Vishal stops his car outside the train station at Railway Feeder Road and yanks the hand brake up. Sitting beside him is his wife and behind are his daughter and Sanjay. Vishal yanks a lever at the side of his seat and the boot flips open.

Sanjay gets out of the car, takes his luggage out and slams the boot shut.

Mrs. Vishal gets out of the car. "Son, good luck in your job-hunting." She hugs Sanjay. "Call us regularly, please."

"Yes, *Amma*, I will."

Sanjay turns to look at his sister, still sitting in the back of the car. He waves and she waves back.

As Sanjay starts to walk to the entrance of the station, his father hollers after him, "Remember, don't do freaky things! I'll arrange a marriage for you once you're settled in a good job."

Sanjay does not answer, and fifteen minutes later, he boards a train heading to Chennai, 630 km away.

Tirunelveli, Tamilnadu, another three years pass ...

The front garden of Vishal's house buzzes with soft conversations and laughter from guests seated at tables covered with spotless white cloth. Along the perimeter fence of the garden are oil lamps mounted on bamboo poles planted at regular distances from each other.

The caterer's waiters have cleared away the empty plates and bowls, and Mrs. Vishal brings a massive cake with candles out of the house and sets it in front of her husband.

Everybody sings, "Happy birthday to you, Happy birthday to you, Happy birthday to Vishal, Happy birthday to you!"

Face beaming with happiness, Vishal blows the candles to loud applause from his friends, relatives and family. Sanjay is absent. Ever since having gone to Chennai, he has neither phoned nor written to any member of his family.

More food arrives from the kitchen and, as the celebration continues, a taxi stops outside the gate and a woman steps out. Togged up in a knee-length skirt and a tight top with ruffles at the neckline, she has long wavy hair falling down her shoulders and golden earrings. She walks up to Vishal whose eyes span wider in surprise.

The woman extends her hand to Vishal. "Happy birthday, *Appa*."

"*Appa*?" asks Vishal with a pinch of his betel brows "Who're you?"

A smile sculpts the woman's red lips. "I'm your son, Sanjay."

"Arrrrgh!" Vishal screws up his face in horror. "What're you doing here dressed like this?"

"I came to wish you happy birthday, *Appa*! Please accept me as what I am."

"You're disgusting!" Vishal jerks to his feet and his chair topples backward. "Get out!"

"*Appa*, please try to understand me."

"You're not my son!" Vishal wags a trembling finger in Sanjay's face. "I disown you!" Vishal turns to holler at his burly brother seated at the next table, "Vikram, get him out!"

Vikam, a retired policeman, steps toward Sanjay and grabs his wrist and back of the neck. "Uncle, I'm not leaving!" protests

Sanjay. As he struggles with Vikram to free himself of his hold, his wig slips off and drops to the grassy ground! He is wearing crew cut. The guests gasp in shock. Mrs. Vishal and her daughter cover their faces with their hands in shame. A male relative stomps on the wig. A male guest pours liquor over it. A third man torches it with a cigarette lighter. The wig starts to burn.

Sanjay breaks out in a sob. "My wig! My beautiful wig!"

"He's a disgrace to the family!" Vishal clutches at his chest, gasps for breath and collapses to the ground.

A voice yells, "Ambulance! Someone call an ambulance!"

Amidst shrieks and screams, blows land on Sanjay and he is thrown out.

Back to the present...
Gautami takes a swallow of her iced lemon tea. "After that incident, I severed ties with my family."

I lean forward and suck at my Coca-Cola through the straw. "What made you come to KL?"

"My cousin works as a barber here." Gautami cuts a piece of meat off a chicken tandoori drumstick. "I came to visit him." She pops the piece into her mouth.

I clap my hands. *Piak! Piak! Piak!*

"No, no. Both your palms should be flat and you should hit them perpendicular to each other."

I clap again. *Piak! Piak! Piak!*

"Ah, that's right!" Gautami puts down her knife and fork and wipes her lips with a piece of serviette. "Now you can be a *hijra*!"

* * *

The mamasan of Hot Angels Nightclub (not its real name) at Old Klang Road, KL, steps inside the massive VIP Karaoke Room, leaving the door open. She strides to the fortyish man sitting on a settee, stops a few feet from him and nods. "Hello! I'm Mummy Angela!" Smiling, she sits down on the settee, keeping a wide space from him. "How shall I address you?"

Turning his head sideways to face Mummy, the man clasps his hands and rests them on his lap. "I'm Edison." Dressed in a loose collared t-shirt, he has a broad forehead which gives him the look of high intelligence.

Mummy stoops and pulls out a menu from the bottom shelf of the coffee table. "Shall we wait for your friends or do you view my hostesses now?" She hands the menu to Edison.

Edison takes the menu and puts it on his lap. "Let me have first pick."

Mummy claps her hands and hollers, "Come in, ladies! Parade time!"

Four girls whose bodies can stir any man's passion stride inside on heels and stand with their backs against one wall.

"Let me introduce my hostesses." Mummy thrusts an open palm at a long-haired girl with a flared skirt. "Far left is – "

"Err, Mummy, I've a special request."

Casting her gaze at Edison, Mummy squishes her arched brows. "Oh? What's that?"

"Can I see how your girls walk? Minus their heels. From one end of the room to the other."

Surprise seizes Mummy's harsh features. "Is this a joke?"

"I'm serious. I will pay each girl a ten-ringgit tip for the effort."

"That's peanuts to them!"

"Make it twenty."

"Agreed! Mummy, I will choose my hostess based on her gait of walking. Not only that I'll barfine her out."

Mummy swings her gaze to her girls. "Everybody agree?"

"Yeeeeeees!" whoop the girls in a chorus and they move to gather at a corner.

Mummy leans back on the settee. "Thom, you first."

The Vietnamese doll struts with a rolling gait with legs wide apart, executes a pirouette mid-way, ballooning her flared skirt, and stops at the other end of the room.

"See?" Mummy grins like a Cheshire cat. "Hootchie mama style of walking! She's hot and playful!"

Edison remains silent.

"Pimchanok."

The Bangkok bombshell, wrapped in a skin-tight sheath dress that reveals her curves, walks like she's treading on a straight line, feet almost shuffling, head held high and ample chest thrust forward.

"Aaaah... elegant like a model."

Edison's face remains stony.

"Angelica, your turn."

The busty Pinay pussycat saunters like there's a spring to her heels, feet close together and big butt moving side to side like a duck waddling.

Mummy leans sideways and half-whispers, "Notice her big butt?" She nods her head in apparent praise. "Gait is like jello on springs – to borrow a movie quote."

Edison leans back in his seat and clucks his tongue.

"Siao Qing!"

Both hands propped on her hips, the tall China doll strolls

like a wading bird, each step a pale shadow of a goosestep that reveals milky thighs in the high slit of her cheongsam.

"Oooooh...Poetry in motion!" Mummy winks. "She's a classy girl."

Edison turns sideways to face the mamasan. "Mummy, why don't you show me the way you walk?"

Mummy's gnarled hand flies to her chest. "Me?"

"Why not?" Edison arcs an eyebrow.

A rumble of ooh's and aah's erupts from the hostesses.

Smiling to reveal horsey teeth, Mummy Angela rises from the settee, kicks off her wedges and takes her position at one end of the room. She glides across the room with smooth steps and a rocking motion to her broad hips.

"Yes!" Edison points a finger at the mamasan. "You're the woman for me! I'm booking you for tonight!"

Ajay, the twentyish bartender, grabs the shaker with both hands as he ends his story. "So, in the end, Edison took Mummy Angela out after our club closed." He starts to shake the shaker with up-and-down motions.

Leaning against the bar, I stomp a cockroach near my shoe. "But why did he choose the mamasan?"

Ajay pours the contents of the shaker into a glass. "Edison told Mummy Angela that research by a sexologist has discovered that a certain way of walking by a woman indicates a high level of vaginal orgasmic ability."

"Who's the sexologist?"

Ajay puts a coaster in front of me. "Dr. Stuart Brody of the University of the West of Scotland." He puts the glass of cocktail on the coaster.

I pull out my wallet and fish out a money note. "No kidding?" I punk it on the bar counter. "Keep the change."

"His research paper was published in the *Journal of Sexual Medicine*, September 2008 issue. The research indicates that a certain stride length and a particular movement of hips reveal a healthy history of vaginal orgasm. Such women perform better in bed."

I scratch the back of my head. "Well, I'll be ..." I take a sip of my cocktail.

My money and Ajay disappear.

Undercover Series

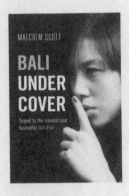